Samuel B. Collins

**Theriaki and their last Dose**

Letters of Fitz Hugh Ludlow and others to Dr. Samuel B. Collins

Samuel B. Collins

**Theriaki and their last Dose**
*Letters of Fitz Hugh Ludlow and others to Dr. Samuel B. Collins*

ISBN/EAN: 9783337135959

Printed in Europe, USA, Canada, Australia, Japan

Cover: Foto ©ninafisch / pixelio.de

More available books at **www.hansebooks.com**

# THERIAKI

AND

# THEIR LAST DOSE.

Letters of Fitz Hugh Ludlow

AND OTHERS, TO

## DR. SAMUEL B. COLLINS,

RELATING TO

THE MOST WONDERFUL MEDICAL
DISCOVERY OF THE AGE.

CHICAGO
EVENING JOURNAL PRINT, NO. 46 DEARBORN STREET
1870.

# AN ANSWER
## TO
## "WHAT SHALL THEY DO TO BE SAVED?"

———o———

FITZ HUGH LUDLOW, in one of his brilliant articles in *Harper*, says:—"A patient, whom, after habitual use of Opium for ten years, I met when he had spent eight years more in reducing his daily dose to half a grain of Morphia, with a view to its eventual complete abandonment, once spoke to me in these words:—'*God seems to help a man in getting out of every difficulty but Opium. There you have to claw your own way out, over red-hot coals, on your hands and knees, and drag yourself by main strength through the burning dungeon bars.*'"

The discovery of a sure Antidote for Opium has been the object of many years of careful research by some of the most eminent physicians of all lands;— but though they had ranged through the wide field of *materia medica*, and exhausted almost every resource known to Science, their labors were not crowned with success.

Flattering hopes had, ever and anon, been flung out to the agonizing thousands of those whom Opium was rapidly dragging down to the grave; to the thousands who had, all unwittingly been drawn by the fatal allurements of the accursed drug into that hell already prepared for them, *lying just beyond life, and just this side of the grave;*— a hell from which escape seems impossible, for *even death is denied them ;*—but they have been as the light of the *Ignis Fatuus,* which shines only to deceive.

But in the mysterious dispensation of an overruling Power, it has been the fortune of an humbler disciple of Esculapius, groping blindly 'n the darkness, but praying earnestly for the light, to find in answer to his prayer, the secret so long hidden — the object of the search of so many years.

How in reality, did he see all around and beside him, the agonized, upturned faces of those for whom there was *no* salvation ; how harshly sounded in his ears the clanking of those chains which no power save the hand of Death could loosen ; and how, as he dreamed of the future, did he see the shackles struck from those millions of slaves — how sweetly sounded in his ears the hallelujahs of the *saved !*·

———o———

In the remedy of Dr. Collins can be found a speedy and a sure relief for the Opium Eater — a certain and a perfect cure — accomplished without pain and without inconvenience.

There need be no interruption of the usual transactions of business, during the treatment —

the Antidote serving, for the time being, as a perfect substitute for Opium — and finally removing entirely any desire for the drug in any form.

Nor does the Antidote in any way induce a habit of relying upon its sustaining power for a single instant after the need for Opium has disappeared.

In short:

> It entirely, and without pain, removes the desire for Opium in any of its numerous forms — or for any substitute for Opium whatever;
>
> It builds up the system, no matter how low it may have been brought by the use of Opium;
>
> And, It leaves the patient as nearly as may be in the same condition as when he first took into his system the deadly poison.
>
> It is not a *patent medicine* but is compounded expressly for the patient for whom it is prescribed, and upon a full statement of his case;
>
> It is not a Panacea. It is designed and adapted only for the cure of the Opium Habit, and is not represented as curing any other disease or habit;

And It is not, in the common acceptation of that word, a Substitute for Opium — it is an *entire cure.*

While effecting the cure, the Antidote takes the place of Opium, and insures the patient against any pain, until he shall be able to forswear Opium altogether, and feel no desire whatever for it, or any substitute therefor.

There are few cases of the Opium Habit so confirmed that the Antidote of Dr. Collins will not cure without suffering, in from 6 to 20 months. It is true there *may* be cases, which, from the complication of other diseases with the disease of Opium Eating, may require a somewhat longer period — but such cases are very rare.

Persons desiring treatment are required to state

1. The exact amount of the drug used weekly;
2. Whether Gum Opium, Morphia, Laudanum, or preparations of Opium in other forms;
3. The number of doses per day, and at what hours taken;
4. What disease, if any, caused them to form the habit;
5. The present condition of health;
6. Sex;
7. Age;
8. Occupation;
9. Daily habits of life;

And upon this diagnosis the Remedy is prepared, and expressly for that particular case; the length of time required for a cure frankly given to the person, and a *cure guaranteed* when all orders of the Doctor are promptly carried out.

It should be remembered that upon the *truth as regards the amount of Opium used*, depends in a great degree, the efficacy of the Antidote

———o———

It will be advisable for patients to order five or six bottles of the medicine at a time, as by that means they save express charges, and avoid the danger of getting entirely out of the Antidote before they can receive more. Each bottle will last *one* month, if taken according to directions.

———o———

Under *no circumstances whatever* should any person taste of the medicine prepared for any patient — nor should any patient take or even taste of any medicine prepared for another patient.

A patient, while under treatment, should avoid vinegar and all other acids, and if, at any time acid fruits should be eaten, they should be well sweetened; — and *all spirituous liquors should be carefully avoided.*

Only when all directions are carefully followed, is a cure guaranteed.

## TERMS.

It has often occurred that Opium Eaters who have been referred to those whom the Antidote has cured, have *ordered their medicine through those parties* — supposing, perhaps, that it would *expedite its delivery* and *lessen its price*. And it has come to the knowledge of Dr. Collins, that in several instances, *those patients have been* COMPELLED TO PAY ONE HUNDRED PER CENT MORE THAN THE DOCTOR HAS CHARGED. For example : — Mr. F. of Michigan, ordered, through a *reference* of the Doctor's residing in the East, five bottles of medicine, for which the Doctor charged FIFTY DOLLARS. After a great deal of circumlocution the medicine arrived, and cost the patient — as per letter now on file — ONE HUNDRED DOLLARS. To avoid this wrong — and to avoid many delays and misunderstandings — the Doctor has advised all patients, when ordering medicine, to *order directly from him*.

Below is appended a scale of prices —

Patients using
| | | |
|---|---|---|
| 1 grain Morphia per day | $6,00 | per month. |
| 3 " " " " | 8,00 | " " |
| 6 " " " " | 10,00 | " " |
| 10 " " " " | 15,00 | " " |
| 15 " " " " | 18,00 | " " |
| 20 " " " " | 20,00 | " " |
| 30 " " " " | 21,00 | " " |
| 40 " " " " | 25,00 | " " |
| 50 " " " " | 28,00 | " " |
| 60 (1 drachm) " " | 30,00 | " " |

Patients using Gum Opium, Laudanum, Elixir of Opium, or other preparation of the drug, must state *explicitly* the amount of *either* — and they will be charged according to its equivalent in Morphine.

All bills payable monthly *in advance*, by draft on some National Bank, or Post Office order.

While Dr. Collins fully appreciates the motives which actuate many of those who are rescued from the terrible and certain fate of the Opium Eater, in making known to suffering humanity at large the sure way of their salvation; — and while he refers with pleasure the Opium Eater to them by name, expecting them to make all inquiries with regard to the truth of that which lies so near their hearts — he has found, that in *justice to himself,* — *and in justice to his patients,* NO ORDERS FOR MEDICINE SHOULD PASS THROUGH THIRD HANDS, but should be addressed DIRECTLY TO HIM.

This will always insure the speedy personal attention of the Doctor, and will protect *him* as it will protect *them* against *many errors,* and perhaps MISREPRESENTATIONS.

All communications are *strictly confidential* — *as are also all names* — when requested, and all letters of inquiry and all orders for medicine will be promptly answered and attended to.

Address, enclosing stamp for return postage,
DR. SAML. B. COLLINS,
LaPorte,
LaPorte County,
P. O. box, 166.          Indiana.

———o———

Dr. Collins refers to any citizen of LaPorte whose own standing in society is good, regarding his private character and his public standing.

———o———

That the Opium Eater *can be cured without suffering* — regardless of the amount of Opium which may have been used, and regardless of the length of time to which the patient may have been addicted to the habit — I subjoin the following mem-

)randa of the amount of the drug used monthly )y a few of my patients whose names I have been cindly permitted to use.

I also present a few of the many certificates of :ures, which I have permission to publish, and I 1ereby offer a reward of Five Hundred ($500) Dollars for the discovery of a single fictitious 1ame among any to which I may refer.

———o———

A. P. Andrew, Jr., LaPorte, Ind.  Habit of 20 years standing.  Used 2 lbs. Laudanum per month.

J. C. Darrow. Adrian, Mich.  Habit of 6 years standing.  Used 270 grains of Morphia per month.

D. Chapman, Chicago, Ill.  Habit of 14 years standing.  Used 540 grains Morphia per month.

Dr. J. H. Clark, Chicago, Ill.  Habit of about 20 years standing.  Used 600 grains Morphia per month.

Mr. W., (No permitted to use name.)  Habit of 8 years standing.  Used 900 grains Morphia per month.

W. W. Culver. Bluff Point, N. Y.  Habit of 20 years standing.  Used 1040 grains Gum Opium per month.

Mr. L., (Not permitted to use name.) Time not known. Used 1500 grains Morphia per month.

———o———

## TESTIMONIALS.

A. P. Andrew, Jr., of LaPorte, LaPorte Co., Ind., deposeth and saith: That he is sixty-eight years of age — that previous to July, 1868, he was for twenty years addicted to the use of Opium, the last eighteen years of which he was confirmed in the Habit. That on the 18th day of July, 1868, he commenced taking a Substitute compounded by Dr. S. B. Collins, of LaPorte — that he continued to take the Substitute according to directions, until the 13th of December following, when he was pronounced cured. That since which time he has not taken Opium in any of its forms, nor any substitute therefor — that he feels no desire or necessity for the use of Opium — that he feels entirely cured of the Habit, with good appetite, sleeps well, and his general health is as good as he could expect at his age — that he published in the *Banner of Light,* Boston, March 13, 1869, a more particular statement of his cure — and that he has no pecuniary interest whatever in the cure, but makes this deposition voluntarily, for the benefit of humanity.   A. P. ANDREW, JR.

Sworn and subscribed to before me, the undersigned Justice of the Peace, this 10th day of August, 1869.

HARVEY BROWN, *Justice of the Peace*

## A CARD

ADRIAN, MICH., April 26, 1868.

DR. SAML. B. COLLINS—*Dear Sir:* Cheerfully will I comply with your request to inform you how I progress in the cure of the Opium Habit. It is now nine days that I have used your medicine, and have worked every day since I returned home from LaPorte, and have not taken a particle of Morphine since I took the first dose of your medicine. I have not suffered any rheumatic pains or felt anyways uneasy, and have been enabled to sleep as calmly and peacefully nights as I ever did in my life.

As it is my sincere wish that you will cause this to be published, for the benefit of those who are suffering with this horrible habit, I will state that I have been a *slave* to the habit of using Morphine for six of the longest years I ever experienced. The last year or two I have taken from eight to ten and twelve grains of Morphine per day, enough to destroy life in the same number of persons. If I omitted taking Morphine one day, I would become completely prostrated and nerveless, would have a flushing and burning sensation one moment, and be completely chilled the next; there are no words in the English language suitable to express the feeling to one not in the Habit, or what I have had to endure when I tried to abstain from taking the drug. During the last three or four years I have consulted several physicians of extensive practice, and have tried many Nervines, Tonics and Stimulants that I thought would benefit me, but found nothing that would even answer as a substitute, much less a cure, until I tried Dr. Collins' treatment.

I had tried so many different remedies and failed, that I had become completely discouraged, and had given up in despair, thinking there was no cure for this accursed Habit. I had not a particle of faith in any remedy. But thanks to Dr. Collins, he has discovered a Cure, and it may be justly considered the most wonderful discovery of this or any other age, for he is the only doctor up to the present time I have heard of who has discovered a cure for any person who has become confirmed in the Opium Habit. It will take eight months to entirely eradicate the effects of the Morphine from my system and restore my health; but I have felt enough better, by using his medicine one week, to amply repay me what he charges if it was nothing but a substitute. I will further state that I never saw Dr. Collins until I went to LaPorte to be examined for this Habit, but what I did see and hear of him leads me to consider him a straightforward, conscientious, honest man, and am confident he will do all that he promises to do in his advertisement.

JOSEPH C. DARROW

## HOPE FOR THE SLAVE.

ADRIAN, MICH., July 4, 1869.

EDITORS LAPORTE ARGUS: For over six years I was a slave to the Habit of using Morphine, with not a ray of hope of ever being emancipated, until I commenced using Dr. Saml. B. Collins' wonderful discovery for the Opium Habit. I have been under his treatment eleven weeks, have not used a particle of Morphia since I commenced taking his medicine, and have been able to work most of the time. I have visited him twice in the eleven weeks, and conversed with those he has cured, (and those who are being cured,) and found them all highly pleased, and perfectly satisfied that the Doctor has done, and will do, all that he advertises to do. I sincerely hope all those who are addicted to this soul-destroying Habit, will avail themselves of this, their only hope, and try his wonderful Remedy which is destined to astonish the whole medical faculty — in fact, the whole world. Patients, in most cases, by following his directions strictly can be cured at their homes, without visiting the Doctor, as he can send medicines by express.

JOSEPH C. DARROW.

———o———
### CURED

Joseph C. Darrow, formerly of Adrian, Lenawee Co., Michigan, now of LaPorte, LaPorte Co., Ind., deposeth and saith: " That he is thirty-five years of age — that previous to April 18, 1869, he had been addicted to and confirmed in the Habit of using Morphine for six years. That on the 18th day of April he commenced taking the Remedy lately discovered, and prescribed by Dr. S. B. Collins, of LaPorte — that he commenced taking the Remedy according to directions, until the 15th of November following, when he was pronounced cured. That since Nov. 15th he has had Morphine at his command, with no necessity or desire to use it, or any substitute therefor; that he feels entirely cured of the Habit, with good appetite, sleeps well, and his health is improving daily.

JOSEPH C. DARROW.

Subscribed and sworn to before me this 27th day of Nov., A. D. 1869.

HARVEY BROWN, *Justice of the Peace*

---o---

LAPORTE, IND., July 30, 1869.

DR. COLLINS — *Dear Sir:* I noticed a letter from A. P. Andrew, Jr., of this city, in one of your weekly newspapers in regard to Opium Eating, and being addicted to the Habit I was induced to try the medicine prescribed by you.

I will state that for the last eighteen years I have been constantly in the use of Opium in different forms, and for the last two years I have used two and a half drachms of Morphine per week.

I commenced taking your medicine the 8d of

May, 1869, and up to this date, I have had no desire to use Opium in any form. Since I began taking your medicine I have not suffered any pain, and my general health has improved, sleep well, and have a good appetite. Before taking the above medicine, I had applied to different members of the Medical Faculty, and tried all the antidotes I could find in medical works, all of which did me no good.

Since I have been taking the medicine I have seen a number of persons whom you have cured, and others who are being cured.

\* \* \* \*

---

## THE OPIUM HABIT.

Oregon, Holt Co., Mo., Nov. 10, 1869.

Editor Chicago Journal — *Sir :* I desire to publish to the world my observations in one case, wherein a person who has been addicted to Opium Eating, has been cured of the Habit, without any suffering whatever. On the contrary, the patient has assured me repeatedly that from the first day that he abandoned the use of Opium and began to use the Remedy, he has been in better health and spirits than he ever was during the time of using the Opium.

During the last four years he has used from two to four drachms of Morphine per week. From two hundred pounds weight he fell to one hundred and fifty pounds ; for five years he had not a natural operation of the bowels, and it required enormous quantities of physic to have any effect. His color was that of a dead person, his eyes glassy and sleepy. In short, *Opium Eater* was branded on his countenance as plainly as it ever was on that of any one. He could not fix his attention five minutes on a book, without going to sleep. He was rapidly advancing to the last stage of Opium Eating. Frequently he tried to reduce the dose, but the less the dose the more stupid he became, and the more obstinate the constipation of the bowels. When the doses became considerably reduced, he had not energy enough to do business. He had no appetite for food, save at breakfast, just after his morning's dose of from fifteen to twenty grains of Morphine.

Hearing that Dr. Saml. B. Collins of LaPorte, Ind., had discovered a Remedy for the Habit, by which he professed to effect a complete cure without any pain or suffering whatever, and having satisfied myself by inquiries that several persons had been cured, I advised him to try it.

I should have stated that he had several times tried to relinquish the Habit, but endured such awful agony at each attempt, that it was more than human nature could persist in. He seemed to have no confidence in any remedy, but was finally prevailed on to try this one. He said that if he felt the least pain or inconvenience, he would resume the use of Morphine, for that he would prefer to die at once than to endure in any degree the torments of an abandonment of the habit. A bottle of the medicine was procured, the regular dose of Morphine was omitted, until he began to suffer from the want of it, and one dose of the Remedy was tried. In two minutes he exclaimed: " That medicine has hit the very spot; I believe in it."

Two days afterward, he met me, and said to me: " I have found a cure at last; I have not touched Opium in any shape for three days. I inquired if he felt sure that there was no Opium in the Remedy. " Look at me and see," he exclaimed. On inspection, I found that his color was much improved, his eyes had a natural expression. This was nearly three months ago. All the marks of Opium Eating have disappeared from his countenance. The organs of the body all perform their natural functions. From the very first day that he tried the Remedy he has pursued his daily business; light has returned to his eye, and color to his cheek.

The case has been under my observation daily from the beginning, and I am satisfied that the Remedy does just what is claimed for it, *viz:* — " cures the Opium Habit without the slightest pain or inconvenience."

That heretofore there has been no hope for the Opium Eaters, that their sufferings consequent on an abandonment of the drug " are unparalleled in the universe," all who have witnessed, must admit. Hence, I consider this one of the greatest discov-cries in our century. As it is but little known, I should like to assist in spreading abroad a knowledge of the fact that such a Remedy has been found. I have only its effects in this one case, yet from its operation, and the peculiar character of the case, I feel confident it will operate as a cure of the Habit in all.

If my confidence is well-founded, then, indeed, we have a triumphant answer to the question so triumphantly argued by Dr. Ludlow, in a last year's number of *Harper's Magazine*, "What Shall They Do to Be Saved?" It will afford me pleasure to assist in giving information to any who may inquire. Respectfully,

MATTHEW SAVILLE, M. D.

———o———

### THE OPIUM HABIT CURED.

#### COMMUNICATION FROM W. W. CULVER.

In this unparalelled age of reform has already been greater and more important discoveries to benefit and ameliorate the condition and wants of humanity than in all recorded previous time. To one especial instance I beg to advert. It is the remedy of Dr. S. B. Collins, of La Porte, Indiana, for the OPIUM HABIT.

I should be dealing unkindly with my sympathetic nature to forego an opportunity to make public my testimony as an actual expert or demonstrator of the infallible efficacy of Dr. Collins' treatment for the expulsion of the destructive habit of Opium Eating, and the use of the drug in any known form. If there lives a person who has suffered what I have from the use of Opium, who could feel indifferent to the misery of others under like suffering, or who would be slow to sound a timely note of alarm to the uninitiated, or point a means of salvation for the already enslaved victim, I can think of no punishment better adapted to such an one than to subject him again to the afflictions of the habit.

Almost twenty years ago I was addicted to the daily use of Opium, and, but for the timely intelligence of the discovered remedy of Dr. Collins, should this day still be an Opium Eater, or have sought release from the enthrallment by voluntary suicide. Dr. Collins is the only man known in the history of the world who ever obtained a victory over the terrible enslavement of Opium. Under no other treatment was a patient ever cured of the habit without enduring suffering which not one organization in a hundred could endure unimpaired, if at all, and never one who would pass through the ordeal a second time for the wealth of the world.

I speak with the authority of experience in this matter, having made it a subject of demonstration; and yet I can conceive of no one capable of being less credulous in relation to the discovery of an antidote for the habit than I was when the fact was first announced by advertisement in a public journal; for I had been using every expedient against the habit on which I could predicate a rational hope of success, and expended time and money at several expensive infirmaries, claiming to treat successfully the habit, and been baffled in every undertaking for relief. I examined all the published authorities on the subject, but found nowhere anything to encourage my hopes, but, on the contrary, ascertained to my satisfaction that there had never been a cure effected greater than one in a hundred could endure and live.

Having received such evidence from the Doctor's patients as no one worthy of cure could doubt, in the month of December, 1869, I left a comfortable home and traveled over five hundred miles to visit the Doctor, then beginning to be esteemed as my prospective savior. On the 21st of the month I had satisfied myself of the genuineness of the Doctor's practice. In the office he occupied I took the first dose of the antidote, from which time to the present I have used in no form one particle of Opium, nor have I felt a desire for it, nor any actual suffering from its disuse, and nothing more than a transient uneasiness once or twice.

It is now four months and four days since I abandoned the habit, and I truly aver that during the time I have felt decidedly better than while indulging the habit. I should already have discontinued the use of the Antidote, but that the

Doctor advised me to continue its use a few weeks. I feel no desire or use for either Opium or the Antidote at this time, and consider myself cured. I seem to be transported into a new and more delightful sphere of existence than I have known for a series of past years. I find beauties, endearments and enjoyments, where, under the abnormalities I was suffering, I saw nothing to cheer my despondency. The elements that surround me all impart a new inspiration and present a changed aspect. I am stimulated into the exercise of a new ambition, and, finally, "old things seem passed away, and all things are become new."

In consideration of the fact that during the last two centuries the medical faculty have exhausted their skill in the search for a remedy for the horrible suffering from the Opium habit, without pretense of success, I may well allude to the discovery of Dr. C. as standing pre-eminent among modern discoveries in the field of therapeutics and *materia medica*.

While at La Porte to visit the doctor, I saw there, one of his first patients, who had been cured for nearly a year, whose experience, as related in detail, was identical with that attending my own. The medicine is a liquid decoction, and not nauseous or much unpleasant to use—not more so than Opium or Morphine—and can be conveniently forwarded, by express or otherwise.

If the foregoing details of Opium Cure induce

any unhappy victim to seek relief by the easy process of regeneration I am now enjoying, or should the uninitiated be put on their guard against the insidious seductions by which the habit is formed, I will have received a satisfactory requital for my pains.

     W. W. CULVER,
      Bluff Point, Yates Co., N. Y.
*April* 25, 1870.

———o———

D. CHAPMAN, & CO.,
  FORWARDING AND COM.,
    FOOT WABASH AVE.,
     CHICAGO, June 26, 1870.

DR. S. B. COLLINS—*Dear Sir:* I feel that I owe you an obligation which I shall never be able to pay, and therefore take this course to acknowledge it. One year ago the 24th day of April, I put myself under your treatment for the habit of using Morphine, which I had used constantly for fourteen years and was a perfect slave to the terrible habit and supposed I always would be as I could get no relief from the best physicians; but from the very first dose I took of your Medicine I had no desire for Morphine, nor did I suffer half as much as I did for the want of Morphine when I was taking that habitually. I never lost a day at my business, and my health was good all the time I was under your treatment, which was up to about the first of December, last, when I left off taking anything and am now all right and take no more Morphine. If you wish to use my name as a reference you are welcome to do so and I will be glad to tell any that may come my experience as a Morphine Eater, for I believe I can sympathize with any one that is so unfortunate as to have such a habit.

Yours truly,

D. CHAPMAN.

———o———

## TO OPIUM EATERS,
### EXPERIENCE OF ONE ADDICTED TO THE HABIT.

ST. JAMES, Mo., Jan. 20, 1870.

EDITORS HERALD: Will you please, for humanity's sake, give this letter one insertion in your valuable and widely-circulated paper?

I have been a practicing physician in the city of St. Joseph for near twenty-three years, during which time I have done a very large practice, and I would say, (not flattering myself,) have some reputation as a physician in Northwest Missouri. About four years ago, I fell into the unfortunate habit of taking Opium. After using the drug that length of time, (four years), it began to tell on my health considerably. I would at one time have given thousands of worlds to have got rid of the miserable habit. I tried some half a dozen times to break off the habit, but failed in every instance, so I had pretty much given up all hopes of recovery.

About this time, December 16th, 1869, I

learned, through my friend Gen. Bassett, of this city, that there was a physician in La Porte, Ind., Dr. S. B. Collins, who put up a Substitute for the Opium Habit, and like a drowning man catching at a straw, I resolved to try the remedy at once; and I do declare, before God and man, that from the first dose of the Remedy, I have not had the least disposition or desire to take Opium in any form whatever, nor did I suffer any of those indescribable, horrid, melancholy feelings which an Opium Eater experiences after stopping the use of the drug. I have now been using the Remedy six weeks. When I first commenced the use of it, I was under the necessity of taking from five to six teaspoonfuls a day; now I only require one teaspoonful in the twenty-four hours, just before going to bed, and I have no doubt that in two or three weeks more I can dispense with the Remedy altogether. I look upon it as one of the most remarkable discoveries of the age, and the greatest boon that God ever gave to the unfortunate Opium Eater. If there are any Opium Eaters in this city or its vicinity, (and I doubt not but there are a few,) if they will call at my office, I will take pleasure in telling them all I know about this wonderful Remedy, and how promptly it has acted in my case.

I would here most positively state and affirm that I have no interest, pecuniarily, in this Medicine, never having seen Dr. Collins in my life.

The reason, and the only reason in writing this letter is, that it may be the means of saving some poor unfortunate person who has become a slave to the accursed thralldom of the Opium Habit. I would to God that all the newspapers in the city, yea, in the United States, would publish and copy this letter, if it would thereby be the means of saving one poor unfortunate person from the miserable and unfortunate habit of Opium Eating.

JNO. B. HOWARD, M. D.

P. S.—It might be proper to state that when I began the use of the drug, I weighed 220 pounds; during the use of the drug I lost about forty pounds in weight, but now, thank God, I am gaining rapidly in health, strength, and flesh. My appetite is good, my digestion is perfect, and I rest well of nights.    J. B. H.

A few months later a letter was received from Dr. Howard, stating that he was completely and permanently cured, but the letter has been mislaid, and cannot be found.

———o———

[FROM THE LOWELL (MASS.) COURIER.]
### TO OPIUM EATERS.

In this paper can be found Dr. S. B. Collins' circular, addressed to all that are or have been in the habit of using Opium in any of its different forms. All that is stated by those that have been cured and that are being treated by Dr. Collins, and more particularly what his patients say of his

Antidote, I know from experience to be true. I would say that for more than six years, prior to July 17th last, I had been a slave to the constant use of Morphine—I had increased its use from one-fourth of a grain to ten and twelve grains per day. Language would fail me were I to attempt to describe the misery and agony that I experienced for the last two years, and more especially for the last six or eight months, prior to the date indicated. I had sought advice and cure from the best and most eminent physicians in the country, an antidote I plead for, from them all, but plead in vain. I then sought consolation in books that gave the experience of Opium Eaters, De Quincy and Coleridge in particular; in fact every book that I could find, that gave the experience of Opium, Morphine, Laudanum, Elixirs, etc.; but the more I read the more miserable I became, as I found that none of the authors had been cured or enabled to give up their favorite drug. By mere accident I heard that Dr. Collins had discovered an Antidote. I wrote to him, and several prominent men and officials of the town, (in which the Dr. lived), from whom I learned that he was a man of integrity in every sense of the word, and that his Discovery or Antidote had performed several remarkable cures. I sent $25.00 to the Doctor, with a request that he would send me its value in his Antidote, which I received July 17th last. I did not feel much confidence in it, but to my surprise, from the first tea-spoonful I took of it, I was relieved from the indescribable, horrible, terrible agony that Opium Eaters know so well, but cannot describe, and have not tasted nor craved Opium in any of its different forms since. I have not lost a meal nor an hour's sleep since by reason of leaving off the drug. My general health has improved, my appetite is better, and in fact I almost feel myself in a new world. I never knew or heard of anything so very wonderful in its beneficial effects, and cannot say enough in its favor. To all who have been so unfortunate as to have contracted the use of Opium in any form, I would say lose not a day, but send to Dr. Collins and give him your age, the length of time you have used it, and the quantity you take per week or day, and get his Compound; and just as sure as you follow his directions, (which are very simple), just so sure will you be cured, and bless the day you first heard that there was an Antidote for the alluring drug.

\* \* \* \*  HENRY READ.

LOWELL, Mass., Nov., '69.

Mr. FITZ HUGH LUDLOW, New York,

*Sir:*—I beg leave herewith to submit to your kindly notice this little Pamphlet of mine, containing, as you will see, your own Correspondence, and a few extracts from the many letters of Mr. Henry Read, bearing upon the subject of my DISCOVERY for the CURE of the OPIUM HABIT.

As these letters — your own as well as Mr. Read's—were private letters—that is, not written with a *view* to *their publication*—my thus giving them this wide publicity, requires, perhaps, an explanation from me.

Personally, no man could invest a private letter with a greater degree of sacredness than do I— and while I most firmly insist that my *rights* in this matter of the *Opium Cure* have been *utterly disregarded;* while the honor of my discovery has not been given to whom it is due; while I have been *wronged by design* out of that of which *every* laborer is *worthy;* and while in *self defense* I have been *driven* to this *dernier resort,* I have not, I assure you, listened so much to those personal promptings of pride and of self interest, as I have to what I firmly believe to be the voice of an *imperative duty which I owe to Humanity*

Separated widely as we may be, you and I, Sir, still hold in common a love for the human race;

my heart as well as your own goes out toward the suffering and the weak: we still hold in common a veneration for the right.

Our common love for suffering humanity was the ground upon which we met—I am sure we shall never part because either fails in his veneration for, or his championship of the right.

Your own letters—Mr. Read's letters—and the facts in the case are before you, and I am sure you will see the great wrong that has been done.

Your article in *Harper* admits of but one interpretation—that *you* had *accomplished*, in the discovery of an Antidote for Opium, the life-long object of your search. The article, viewed, however, in the light thrown upon it by your letters, shows a capability of a much different rendering.

The *specific* discovery to which you referred, or *promised to refer*, was so *carefully concealed* that your "NOBLE HEARTED AND PHILANTHROPIC FRIEND, MR. HENRY READ, OF LOWELL, MASSACHUSETTS," to whom in your article you gave such prominence, *availed himself of his opportunity to turn an honest penny by representing the article to have been written in behalf of a supposed Antidote discovered by a man by the name of Stillman.* The wrong which might thus have been done to thousands of Opium Eaters who rely upon the conscientiousness of *your* opinion is incalculable.

Either all this was pursuant to an understanding between youself and your "agent," Mr. Read—which I cannot believe—or Mr. Read in endangering the reputation of his friend, has assumed a tremendous responsibility for which he should be made to answer.

As between you and him, however, I have nothing to do—my only object being to thus briefly lay the matter before you, not doubting that your sense of justice will dictate to you the proper course to be pursued.

I am, Sir, respectfully,

SAMUEL B. COLLINS.

———o———

18 WEST 14TH ST., NEW YORK, }
Nov. 25, 1869.

DR. S. B. COLLINS—*Dear Sir:* It is possible that you may know me by name and have read some of my published writings upon the subject of the Opium Habit—perhaps have even read the book of that name published by the Messrs. Harpers, in which you will then have had a good chance to become acquainted with me. I will only here say that I have for many years made this most painful subject a specialty both of study and treatment—have had, perhaps, a larger circle of acquaintance with Opium Eaters than any one else in this country, and have been so happy as to **cure a considerable number of the worst cases on record**

None of these cases have, however, I frankly acknowledge, been effected without severe and long protracted suffering—although I have been enabled to mitigate the horrors of the trial by the bringing to bear of every faculty upon the judicious selection of palliatives, to an extent which made the agony far less than without my aid it would have been.

But I have all my life been seeking in *vain* for some remedy which would act as a substitute and bring the patient out painlessly. Last spring I was almost ready to give the search up in despair—when two of my large circle of Opium correspondents wrote me within a few weeks of each other that you had succeeded in making the discovery—at least that your circulars positively announced the fact, and that several persons who had had recourse to you had found your assertion remarkably corroborated by their experience.

I can assure you that my heart leapt for joy at the bare possibility of such a thing. I own I should have been glad to have discovered for myself an agent, which, if it does all that you claim for it is one of the *grandest—most beneficent—most glorious discoveries ever made in medicine—*but God knows that my pity for the terrible sufferings I have seen is such that all professional pride utterly sinks out of sight, and I would most gratefully to both God and the discoverer come to learn of any one who could confer such an inestimable boon as your remedy purports to be.

If it does all that I understand to be claimed for it, and is itself no form of extract from the accursed poppy—then you have a *right to the thankful praise—the respect—the honorable tributes of every man who loves his race:—you have made a discovery, not one whit exceeded in importance by Jenner's discovery of vaccination*—one which will quite as justly entitle you to applause, living, and monuments when dead.

*Out* of a *sincere heart* I say this—high praise as it may seem—for the suffering from Opium, in un-numbered cases, I have seen to be greater than that of any other disease or physical torture whatever.

A few weeks ago, one of your patients (who corresponded with me for the first time after he had taken your Remedy), sent me a 2 oz. phial—knowing from my writings that I should feel the truest interest in trying the effect upon Opium Eaters. I happened to have one case in particular just then under my charge, which seemed sometimes almost hopeless from the complication of other difficulties with the Habit of Opium, and I used the small portion of your Remedy which had been sent me, on that case alone—beginning with very small doses, and at several day's interval apart, and not attempting to cut off the patient's Opium, altogether, because I knew I had only enough of your tincture for a very short and incomplete experiment.

My experience of it however, as far as it went, showed me that it possessed some quite remarkable powers. I was able, by its aid greatly to diminish the doses of Morphine and increased the interval between them—and although I had no opportunity to judge whether it would enable me to cut off the Opium altogether, I still saw enough to make me think that possible, and to give me a desire to make the trial on some case like his.

I accordingly resolved to write you and make the following proposition, viz: that you supply me with enough of your discovery to make the complete experiment in one case—and if I find it result as my correspondents have said, I will not only give you my personal thanks, but put you in the immediate receipt of many hundred dollars custom.

As I have already said, I am in constant receipt of a larger number of appeals for help from Opium Eaters than any other man in this country—and have a desk-full of applications now which I could hand over to you and which would most gratefully be answered by your Remedy—had I once a chance of satisfying myself of its exact value. Moreover, my position is such in connection with the press and the Medical Profession, that I possess facilities for making you and your Remedy widely known—such as no other man in the country has. I can make it most immensely for your interest to co-operate with me, if, after the experiment we are convinced that it is for our common good and that of suffering humanity.

At present, I will not go into further details, but will only add that should you need to learn of me further, you can write to Mr. Clarke Irvine, Oregon, Holt Co., Mo., and if you have not got it I will cheerfully send you the "Opium Habit" book.

My only desire is to save Opium Eaters—pecuniary advantage is a most subsidiary consideration—but if there is money to be made out of this Remedy at all, it is but right that you should make it. I hope you will be able to patent your secret, so that you may disclose it to the scientific world without pecuniary loss, for if the Remedy does what is claimed for it, it would be one of the greatest of human calamities to have its mode of preparation die with its discoverer. Oblige me by an early answer, and if you think well of my proposition, express as much of the Remedy as may suffice for the experiment. My direction is "Fitz Hugh Ludlow, 18 West 14th Street, New York."

I am yours, truly,

(Signed) F. H. LUDLOW.

———o———

18 West 14th St., N. Y., Jan. 23, 1870.

DR. S. B. COLLINS—*Dear Sir:* I regret your inability to supply me with the means for making such a test of your remedy as would alone justify any conscientious man of any scientific standing in recommending it. You must see, of course, that if such a man has achieved any position where his good word could be of any value to you, that position would be seriously imperilled by his advising patients to take a remedy of which he himself had no practical knowledge.

Any person who will consent to recommend a remedy blindfold—simply on agreement that he is to receive a percentage for every customer furnished—must necessarily be a person whose opinion is of no consequence one way or the other. I know a number of practioners who would gladly make an arrangement to procure takers for any compound that could be invented, provided only that they were well paid for the use of their names—but I could not advise anybody to invest very largely in their names who was seeking a profitable speculation.

So I think it will be universally found—the man whose influence is weighty and extended, and whose praise really means something when he gives it, is a man who never expresses an opinion where he has not the most ample grounds for it, and who by years of fidelity to scientific tests has earned the reputation of truthfulness, caution, mathematical exactness, experience and skill. So far at least as conscientiousness and wide acquaintance with the subject can make it, my reputation is such an one as this. Whatever good my recommendation and influence would do your remedy,

I have earned the ability to do for it by conscientiously devoting a large portion of my life to the study of the Opium Eater's unhappy condition, and the attempt to discover by what means I could best help or save him—this, not primarily with a view to my own aggrandizement, but because my pity and sympathy for the most agonizing sufferings which humanity is ever called to bear would not let me rest.

If any one values my opinion it is because I have tried to bring to this work all the resources of science, all the ingenuity, all the patience which I possessed—so that when I speak, people will be sure at least that my conclusions are not vitiated by any self interest, but are stated as honestly as if I were advising a brother or a sister, or prescribing for my own case.

Understand me, I do not pretend to deny that the laborer is worthy of his hire—do not mean to say that people who are able ought not to pay and pay handsomely in proportion to their means, for such a salvation as would be comprehended in their rescue from the hell of Opium—more especially when that rescue is painless as yours professes to be.

I think no amount of money can begin to repay the man whose labors have discovered such a salvation as that. I only hope that sometime you will see your way clear to putting it in the power of every one to avail himself of that salvation— as you would be able to do if you got a Patent, and could sell rights everywhere. What a frightful loss to suffering humanity it would be if such a secret should die with you! It seems to me that I should have to come back from another world to declare it, before I could rest. Of course you know the universal unwillingness among physicians to use any medicine which is kept a secret from the profession. I, however, would gladly stretch a point—so deep is my desire that the awful sufferings of the many thousands of Opium Eaters should be relieved—and not demand to know your formula for preparing the compound, nor any of its elements—if I could only have the chance of seeing a patient go through with the trial, I, myself, administering the remedy according to your directions.

Many scientific men would blame me for doing this—but I have no dearer object than the relief of human suffering, and if I find that a given thing does relieve it without bringing worse evils in its own train, I will not refuse to use it until I can understand its *modus operandi*.

So, if I by using your medicine, following your directions strictly, and seeing the result come out satisfactorily under my own conscientious observation can ascertain that this medicine will effectually cure the Opium Habit, I will gladly set people taking it without waiting to find out its composition. Nor need you fear that I would be a prejudiced judge. If you have discovered that most wonderful thing, a painless, even a *comparatively* painless Opium Cure, I am as glad of it—I welcome it as cordially as if I had discovered it myself.

My prejudices are all in its favor—I could never judge it severely—I shall be only too anxious to find it thoroughly fulfil all its promises, will help it in every way, and feel no discouragement nor alarm if any symptoms new to practice, should arise during the process of cure. I know that giving up Opium, involves a most tremendous, upturning, overhauling, reconstruction of the constitution, and am familiar, through countless cases with the appearance of symptoms which any one inexperienced would have thought fatal, and which would have made them at once desist from the effort to save the patient from his hell.

If, therefore, I have a chance to give your remedy a trial, you may be sure that it can not be submitted to any judge fairer toward it—or rather, I should say, more prejudiced in its favor, for I am ready to hail, with open arms, and give the full weight of my influence to anything whatever, that my own eyes have once beheld fulfil the simple requisition of bringing the Opium Eater out, with little or no pain.

As I told you in my last letter, I am in almost daily receipt of letters from Opium Eaters crying for help—people ready to give all they possess for salvation. People are constantly coming to see me—like the letters, some of them from remote parts of the country—ready to do anything if only they can get out of their hell, without suffering so much as to lose life or reason. If I can have your Remedy to try upon a single case—so it can be wholly under my own eyes, yet treated, as to the medicine, according to your directions for its use, and that one case has at all a successful issue—I will instantly see that all the others use it, if you are able to supply it fast enough. I could, this very hour, put you in the way of disposing of thousands of dollars worth of your Remedy, if you had already given me the fair opportunity I ask.

Nobody, I can safely say, could more instantly make your Remedy universal in its demand. I have, as it were, the country full (represented by my desk-full) of customers for you. The work of years is done for you already, if you entrust your Remedy to my hands for a single case. Moreover, if the experiment proves satisfactory, I possess the power by using my pen in any dozen of the many organs of public information open to me, as a literary man no less than a scientific one, to make your Remedy known and clamored for, from every corner of this country, and eventually of the civilized world.

Nothing of this is boasting, but the simple statement of facts which are necessary to be understood between us, for I am seeking not my own aggrandizement but the welfare of sufferers, for whom my whole heart has been interested for years. That those who can afford to pay for help ought to do so—that I expect them to do so—that it is better, both for the benefactor and benefited, that they should do so is beyond question, and whenever you conclude to put the matter in such a shape that we can talk of business, I shall be ready to do so—and you will find me as fair in making arrangements, as I am in seeking the necessarily previous experiment now. My view of the best way for us to co-operate (should we arrive at that purpose) is not yet fully formed, but I have thought that perhaps the best way to enable both of us to be useful to each other and humanity, might be this, viz: that I should secure the means for the establishment of a labratory here in New York, large enough to supply the demand of the whole country, and that you, if you are willing, should come on here and take the entire charge of the manufacture of the Remedy:— I undertaking to manage the entire-work of creating the demand for it—making it known through all the journals and magazines open to me, and, if necessary, publishing a supplement to "The Opium Habit"—a smaller book, to sell at about cost price, and for gratuitous distribution among the most influential practitioners and heads of sanitary institutions—devoted entirely to the enlightenment of the public upon this wonderful new means of cure.

New York is and always must be the business centre, and from here, accordingly, can better be managed the vast system of correspondence and manufacture and shipment, which would be immediately demanded by so thorough an advertising of the Medicine as I propose. If you are not absolutely fastened to La Porte, your removal to New York would be, in a business point of view invaluable to you, and could easily be provided for.

Moreover, your having entire charge of the labratory would keep your secret, if that continues to be an object with you, in your own hands, while the Remedy was still undergoing the widest advertisement—a thing which would be very difficult after it became widely advertised, unless you limited the amount of your manufacture. And that last would be sure to cause a prejudice against it. Here, you could manufacture enough to supply all demands and have unequalled facilities for shipping without entrusting the manufacture to subordinate hands, at minor centres, all over the country. I am not, however, so wedded to this plan that I do more than throw it out for your reflection.

Finally, then, to come to the point that is essential: In your answer to my former note, you say that at that date you had not the facilities for making the Medicine fast enough to supply the customers you already had, but that before long you hoped to be able to send me the first bottle of the series requisite for the experiment I proposed. In a letter from Mr. Darrow, to another gentleman who forwarded it to me—Mr. D. says that you told him you had heard from me and that you were going to send me a package. I have not received any such as yet—but one or two other gentlemen who have been Opium Eaters and need your Remedy, write so earnestly, begging that I would co-operate with you in making known what they regard a great blessing, that I am willing to waive all ceremony and again propose that you should enable me try your Remedy. I shall be very much pleased if it be within your power to send me the Medicine at this time. I have one patient who has used Morphine for several years, and though not an extreme case, is still from the lack of any unfavorable complication a good one to try the Remedy on. I am all the more willing to make the trial with her, because you will have a guarantee that I ask you to furnish your Medicine from no motives of pecuniary selfishness, in the fact that she is in very straightened circumstances, and I shall not charge her for either Medicine or services a single cent. Her case has deeply won my sympathies, and in giving me the Medicine for her you will only be sharing a benevolence with me and not aggrandizing me. Indeed I hope that my friends and I will be able to afford her pecuniary aid beyond her cure.

She is a very refined and well taught woman,

who needs only to be saved to herself to make her own and an infirm mother's living very comfortably. If you write me on the receipt of this that you are willing to furnish the requisite Medicine, I am ready to begin at once and will forthwith forward you a detailed statement of her case which will enable you to prepare the successive bottles, and will, as I have said, see that the Remedy is administered strictly as you say.

Here is as good an opportunity as we shall have to co-operate, and I shall be glad if you will, as early as convenient, reply on the subject to

Yours, very truly,

(Signed)         FITZ HUGH LUDLOW,
18 *West* 14*th Street, New York.*

———o———

18 West 14th St., New York, }
Jan. 26, 1870. }

DR. S. B. COLLINS—*Dear Sir:* According to my last note (though without waiting to receive an answer) I herewith state to you the case of the patient whom I desire to treat with your remedy.

(Here follows the statement of the case.)

\*   \*   \*   I have always found that the length of time during which the patient has been taking Opium is a much more important element than the amount he has reached, in the question of cure.

\*    \*    \*    \*    \*

I do not know of a case among the hundreds I have seen, in which I would go to work with more sanguine feelings in the case of a Remedy which is said to do all yours is, and there is the additional motive to select this for an experiment in the fact that the poor woman is indeed almost utterly destitute, and a most worthy object of benevolence in every respect.

\*    \*    \*    \*    \*

Hoping to hear from you at an early date,
I am yours truly,
(Signed)        FITZ HUGH LUDLOW.

———o———

No. 18 West 14th St., New York, }
Feb. 14, 1870.

\*    \*    \*    \*    \*

But *the value of a Remedy* which does as yours is delared to *is in the salvation of the Opium Eater without the suffering and the absolute cessation from all labor which are necessary with all other means and plans of cure.*

I know that I can cure Opium Eaters and eradicate the Habit thoroughly, but I *frankly acknowledge that I cannot do it without its creating more or less suffering—sometimes even severe suffering to the patient—and taking him for a considerable length of time from his avocations.*

\*  \*  \*  I have sought in all our communications to deal with the utmost fairness and courtesy myself, and I beg that you will not disappoint me.

Yours truly,
(Signed)        FITZ HUGH LUDLOW.

18 West 14th St., April 4, 1870.

\* \* \* I regret to learn that your lungs are diseased. If you will describe your difficulty, I will, (supposing you care to have me), do anything in my power to advise and help you. Your life is now too precious to be lost. I don't wish to appear even to preach, but I must say that I think you possess the most tremendous responsibility which can belong to any man upon the earth, in being the possessor of a Remedy which wisely administered can do so much for the human race.

\* \* \* \* \*

(Signed) FITZ HUGH LUDLOW.

———o———

99 Clinton Place, New York,
April 20, 1870.

\* \* \* When I have time to tell you my proposition (before referred to) you will see that I have a better and much cheaper plan for making your Remedy widely known, than to put into *Harper's* the advertisement you send—which would cost a dollar a line. If you and I agree, *I will publish a letter over my own name in Harper's, calling attention to the fact of a wonderful discovery for the Opium Cure.*

\* \* \* \* \*

(Signed) FITZ HUGH LUDLOW.

———o———

99 CLINTON PLACE, NEW YORK,
May 10, 1870.

S. B. COLLINS—*Sir:* The package of five

bottles for which I last wrote, came duly to hand.

\* \* \* \* \*

I am going to take a very important case under my direct charge—the case of a quite distinguished and eminent man, whose cure will be the greatest of triumphs, and who has used Opium very largely for years. I shall probably, as my own health needs rest and recreation after my many long years of hard work, take a voyage to England with him, and stay in London a number of weeks.

\* \* \* \* \*

If you will furnish me with all the medicine necessary to treat this case—supplying me with a sufficient stock of bottles (say 10 or 12) when I start, to make sure the case should be interrupted by no delays or accidents, at that long distance of London from La Porte—I will put into both *Harper's Weekly and Monthly,* over my own name, two letters publishing your Discovery and its value to the several millions who read those periodicals. In no other way, by paying hundreds for advertising, even, could you reach so many people, or so well. Decide and let me know your answer as early as possible.

Yours,
(Signed)         FITZ HUGH LUDLOW.

99 CLINTON PLACE, NEW YORK,
June 14, 1870.

S. B. COLLINS—*Sir:* Our mutual friend, Mr.

Read, has just been paying me a visit and consulting in regard to some arrangement by which *we* can work together for the benefit of the Remedy and the Opium Eaters.

I have only to say that I have read the proposition he makes you, over *again and again* carefully—and fully approve of it. I stand ready to assist him in every way through the press if you and he make the arrangement. Whatever he says, or may hereafter say, on the subject, I agree to. I give notice now, that he represents *me* in *every business arrangement* with *you* in *my absence*.

I have now put into the Harpers' hands to be published in the very *first* magazine that there is room for it in, *an article recommending your discovery*, that *every body* who has seen it says is *one of the finest things I ever wrote*. *Harper's Magazine* is always printed over a month ahead—so it cannot come out in any shorter time—and I rely upon you to believe me, and wait for it, and not come down on Mr. Read for any money for those 12 bottles until you have given it the proper *chance* and *time* to be published. If you do come down on him for the money—of course I shall at once learn of it by telegraph, and have the article cancelled and not published at all. But I believe you mean to act square.

  *  \*  \*  \*  \*

Truly yours,

(Signed)     FITZ HUGH LUDLOW.

The following extracts are taken from letters *written* and *signed* by Mr. HENRY READ, of Lowell, Mass.

While it is true that they are only *clippings—* and disconnected as such extracts must necessarily be—the reader is assured that *they are verbatim,* and that in no instance have the extracts been so arranged as to *change* in the *slightest,* the *obvious* and *unmistakable meaning* of their *author,* as the original letters now in the possession of the compiler will prove.

———o———

### MR. READ DISCOURSES CONCERNING HIMSELF.

(1.) "I have been indorsed by Secretary Boutwell, our present Secretary of the U. S. Treasury, and several Members of Congress, which, by the way, is *nothing very favorable to any man,* as many of the present Members of Congress are, in my opinion, rather '*small potatoes,*' and *would indorse anybody for pay*—that is, unless they are belied."

(2.) "I have no 'horn to blow,' nor shall I praise myself. But if you care to inquire, you can ask the *Mayor of our city,* the *Presidents* and *Cashiers* of any or all of our Banks here, and of all or any *Official,* or any *prominent man* or *men* here."

(3.) "I can secure the influence of BUTLER, SUMNER, WILSON, DAWES, BROOKS, BANKS, BOUTWELL, and a *majority* of the *Committee of Ways and Means,* if necessary."

(4.) "I am your *friend*, Dr. Collins, and *have* been, ever since the first dose I took of your Compound."

(5.) "For if ever one man tried to help another, *I have tried to help you*."

---o---

## MR. READ DISCOURSES CONCERNING FITZ HUGH LUDLOW, AND PLACES HIM IN A SINGULAR LIGHT.

(6.) "The fact is, the *Doctor* don't want it *known* that he and *I* are intending to make a business arrangement *with you—which*, if made, *must all be in my name*."

(7.) "But before anything is done or agreed upon, *Dr. Ludlow must be away, out of the country, and not be known as an interested party at all*."

(8.) "He, (*Dr. L*.,) *thinks that he better not be known us being an interested party, except as a Philanthropist*."

(9.) "If we come to any agreement, *it must not be known that Dr. L. has any interest in it, save that of Humanity*."

(10.) "The fact is, brother Collins, we must *please* and *keep sweet Dr. L*."

(11.) "Dr. L. thinks he could be of most service *not to be known as a Partner*, but to act in behalf of the Compound, by *recommending* it to Physicians, *upon its merits*."

(12.) Mr. Read, writing from No. 99 Clinton Place, N. Y.,—Mr. Ludlow's address—under date of June 13th—after making a sort of proposition to purchase an interest in Dr. Collins' Discovery, which proposition he claims to have been written by Mr. Ludlow, says in explanation; "and I have copied it, *as he don't want to be known as being interested,* as he can do ten times more good *not to be known* as *being interested* with me, or *in any way interested,* save as a *writer* and '*talker up*' of it in the best literary papers."

### MR. READ DISCOURSES CONCERNING THE SECRET.

(13.) "He, (Dr. Ludlow,) is the only M. D. to whom you need to reveal the *secret* or articles from which it (the Antidote), is compounded."

(14.) "Should you have any trouble in obtaining a *Patent,* he, Dr. L., knows how to manage—and if a scientific man like he is will indorse it the Patent will be granted."

(15.) "If you have, or are likely to have any trouble in getting a *Patent for your Discovery,* I can, with Dr. Ludlow's influence, help you amazingly. I have a *brother-in-law* and *several relatives in Congress.*"

### MR. READ DISCOURSES CONCERNING A PARTNERSHIP.

(16.) "I would advise you by all means to accept of any terms Dr. Ludlow may offer."

(17.) "I do hope that you and Dr. Ludlow will arrange so you can receive his influence and aid."

(18.) "I would come on to La Porte, and see you, if you are disposed to make an arrangement with me and the Doctor that would be *advantageous to us three.*"

(19.) "I will, immediatly after he, (Dr. L.,) is *gone,* make you a good and liberal proposition for a *partnership* or *interest* in your Antidote."

### MR. READ DISCOURSES CONCERNING THE ARTICLE IN HARPER, AND OTHER THINGS.

(20.) "(Dr. L.), says: 'that he *has decided* to write you one or more letters and have them published *over his own name,* in Harper and other New York papers if you will furnish him with the *compound necessary for the cure of one patient* that he is going to take with him to Europe.'"

(21.) "I told you some time ago that Ludlow had written for Harper or some other Magazine or paper—and *he did* so *write,* and *not only* referred to *you* but *your Discovery.* This I know and have seen *extracts from it long and long* before the piece in Harper appeared."

(22.) "The *first article I read* expressly told the public that HE WAS NOT THE DISCOVERER OF THE CURE."

(23.) "I am in daily and hourly receipt of letters from Opium patients that Ludlow's piece is sending me.

His *first article* (that, it seems, you did not see) —*sent me 20 or more letters* from Opium subjects."

(24.) "Dr. L. wrote a *new* piece *yesterday*, (*a splendid one*), and the Harper's will put it in the next issue. It is *really the best article* or *notice* I ever saw written. He, *in this new article*, referred Opium Eaters *in this vicinity* to me—so you will have to send me a lot of medicine at once, and at your *lowest price*, and I will charge *all I can get for it.*"

(25.) "You will be pleased when you see Dr. L.'s article in the *Harper's Monthly.* * * * But such an article as he (Dr. L.,) has written, (*over his own name, too,*) IN FAVOR OF YOUR ANTIDOTE, I never saw written before in its favor."

(26.) "The piece he (Dr. L.,) wrote *last* is the *best* article I ever saw, and you may rest assured it will be inserted and published."

(27.) "I heard the firm, (Harpers), or one of them, say to Dr. L. these words: '*Not for one thousand dollars, Dr. Ludlow, would we give room in our Magazine for your article to any other man than yourself!*'"

(28.) "I will, as soon as I can find time, (from my present hurry), write all those correspondents of Ludlow's, (that don't happen to see his letter in Harper), and tell them to *send for* and take the Antidote—*Ludlow requested me to do so.*"

(29.) "*That you were not referred to by Ludlow in his last letter I cannot and do not understand. Yet he meant or intended no slight*—else why should *his first article refer to you and your locality, and as the Originator and Discoverer of this great Remedy?*"

(30.) "At all events you get the benefit of every word he has said, and if you furnish the Compound for the patients, *wherein are you harmed by* the omission of your name, residence, etc., in Ludlow's last article?"

———o———

### A FEW REMARKS BEARING UPON THE ABOVE EXTRACTS AND THEIR AUTHOR, MR. READ.

Mr. Read comes to us very well indorsed by those who *ought* to know him, (Extracts No. 1 and 2), and he is very *rich* in *Congressional influence*—though he does not value the latter very highly—but a careful examination of his letters—a comparison of his statements with the known facts—and a general knowledge of his acts with regard to the Discovery of Dr. Collins, must impress upon the mind of the reader the belief that those indorsements and that influence, which, in giving, left the donors no poorer, were of inestimable value to Mr. Read—giving him something upon which he might stand, *and without which he would be poor indeed.*

The statement of Mr. Read that he was the *friend* of Dr. Collins, (Extract No. 4), arises either from a child-like innocence of what a friend is and should be—or from a desire to *deceive*—to cover up under the guise of a firm friendship the deep wrong he was doing—for surely no one would say that the facts in the case corroborate his statements.

With an enthusiasm as great as though he were really uttering a truth, he says: (Ex. 5) "For if ever one man tried to help another, *I have tried to help you*"—forgetting, alas, for his poor memory! *that it stands in proof* that he has all along been *playing a double game*—has been *false to Mr. Ludlow—false to Dr. Collins*—and last, let us hope also, least—false to *himself.* He forgets that it is in proof that upon the *face of Mr. Ludlow's article* in *Harper*, he *has recommended other Remedies* for the cure of the Opium Habit, *as being the one referred to by Mr. Ludlow.*

Does the reader fancy Mr. Read *knows more about the suppression of Dr. Collins' name and the insertion of his own in the Harper article*, than he cares to tell? (See Ext. 29.)

Next to the great wrong which Mr. Read has

done to thousands of Opium Eaters, is the grevious wrong he has done to his more than friend, *Fitz Hugh Ludlow.* He has been *trifling* with *something* with *which* he *is not familiar*—the honorable name and fair reputation of a gentleman and a scholar.

While Mr. Ludlow is very desirous of forming a partnership with Dr. Collins, he wishes it to be distinctly understood that it must *not be known that he is an interested party at all*—and all arrangements must be made in the name of *Mr. Read.* (Ext. 6, 7, 8, 9, 11, 12.)

He must be known only as being interested as a PHILANTHROPIST—(Ext. 8)—or for the SAKE OF HUMANITY—(Ext. 9.) True Philanthropists—men who really labor for the sake of humanity—are very hard to find; but it would not take long to flood the market with such noble hearted philanthrophy as that. But what careful reader of the letters of Fitz Hugh Ludlow will believe that the heart that dictated them could be utterly bad—would believe that he, after years of labor to build up for himself an honorable and an enduring name, would hold that name thus lightly—would *sell it to the highest bidder!*

All of Mr. Read's attempts to make himself the confidante of Dr. Collins, having failed, and the longed for secret being still beyond his grasp, he endeavored to persuade the Doctor to *patent his discovery.* Ex. (14, 15.) The casual reader might, perhaps, at once come to the conclusion that Mr. Read's grand idea in offering to help the Discovery to a Patent, was to obtain for himself a knowledge of the secret—but this, the reader is assured would be denied by Mr. Read. He would probably say that it was *for the Doctor's good*—or perhaps for the *good of humanity*—for has not Mr. Ludlow called Mr. Read his " *noble hearted* and *philanthropic friend ?*"

Whether or not Fitz Hugh Ludlow *knew* the man he was honoring by a prominent notice in Harper, the reader may decide.

A Partnership was next strongly urged by Mr. Read (Ext. 16, 17, 18,) but with his usual poor success. He was not so blind but as to see that the Antidote was one which was destined to be known the world over, and perhaps Mr. Read felt that with his influence it would do *much more good to humanity*—for who would dare to say that the noble hearted *philanthropist ever* for a *moment remembered self?*

Does the reader wonder why Mr. Read must needs have delayed the announcement of his proposition until *Mr. Ludlow had left the continent?* (Ext. 19.) For philanthropic reasons?

The article in the Easy Chair of Harper for August, and the misrepresentations regarding it, was the immediate cause of the issuance of this pamphlet—and to that part of Mr. Read's letters bearing upon that subject, the attention of the reader is requested.

Mr. Read says that Mr. Ludlow has decided to write one or more letters for Harper, provided Dr. Collins would send him an amount of medicine sufficient to cure one patient. (Ext. 20.) This *amount of medicine was sent* and *its receipt acknowledged* in *Mr. Ludlow's letter* of *June* 14*th.*

Mr. Read says, (Ext. 21,) that Mr. Ludlow had written an article in which he referred *not only to Dr. Collins but to his remedy*—and that, (Ext. 22) in that article Mr. Ludlow *expressly told* the *public that he, Mr. Ludlow, was not the discoverer of the cure.* Now Mr. Read has been requested *four* different times to give the *name* of the *magazine* or *paper* in which that article appeared—*but he has always avoided an answer.*

Mr. Ludlow's first article (in *which he used* the *name* of Dr. Collins) sent Read 20 or more letters from Opium Eaters (Ext. 23). It never sent Dr. Collins *one letter* a fact that might look very strange *had any one* but *Mr. Read said that such an article ever appeared.*

Extracts No. 24, 25, 26 and 27, were all written before the article in Harper appeared, and the idea which they were intended to convey is patent to the reader.

The " *new* piece" which Mr. Ludlow wrote was " the best article **or** notice he (Mr. Read) ever saw written," and it referred, says Mr. Read, "Opium Eaters in *this vicinity to me.*" The reader is requested to examine the article from Harper and find the words " in this vicinity"—or any words to the same effect.

The reader will observe that this enthusiastic paragraph is closed by an appeal for a *lot* of *medicine* at the Doctor's *lowest price*, and a promise that he (Read) would charge *all* he *could get for it.* This, too, when Mr. Read *knew that every bottle of the Antidote* was compounded *for a particular patient,* and would favorably effect none other.) Mr. Read's philanthropy sometimes carries him to great lengths.

### A RECAPITULATION OF MR. READ'S LETTERS.

Mr. Read says he is *indorsed by Secy. Boutwell.* (Ex. 1)

This gives Secy. Boutwell a large contract.

Mr. Read says he has *no* "*horn to blow,*" himself. (Ex. 2.)

But he nominates those who "blow" for him.

Mr. Read says he can *secure* the *influence of Butler, Wilson, Dawes, Brooks, Banks,* and a *majority* of the *Committee of Ways and Means.* (Ex. 3.)

Upon the principal that misery loves company, this must please Secy. Boutwell.

Mr. Read says he is the friend of Dr. Collins. (Ex. 4.)

This is a *mistake*, as the reader may judge.

Mr. Read says he has *tried* faithfully to *help Dr. Collins.* (Ex. 5.)

The reader may judge of the *truth* of this statement.

Mr. Read says, in effect, that Mr. Ludlow disposes of his *reputation* for *honesty* for a consideration. (Ex. 6, 7, 8, 9, 11, 12.)

*This is for Mr. Ludlow to answer.* The reader, in the *mean time, forming his own opinion.*

Mr. Read says he is anxious that the *Discovery be patented.* (Ex. 14 and 15.)

This is done only from Mr. Read's *Philanthropic desire to benefit humanity.*

Mr. Read says Mr. Ludlow is very anxious to form a co-partnership with Dr. Collins. (Ex. 16, 18 and 19.)

But Mr. Read dare not make any arrangements until Mr. Ludlow leaves for Europe.

Mr. Read says Mr. Ludlow has decided to write an article for Harper. (Ex. 20.)

Knowing positively that Mr. Ludlow *did* finally write an article for Harper, we are inclined to believe that this statement is true.

Mr. Read says Mr. Ludlow wrote an article in which he *referred* to *Dr. Collins* and his *Discovery*—and in which he said that *he*, (*Ludlow*), was not the *discoverer* of the *Cure*. (Ex. 21 and 22.)

Mr. Read has failed to *give* the *name* of the publication in which this article appeared, and so the reader must again judge of the truth of the statement.

Mr. Read says that the *first* article of Mr. Ludlow's,(in which he referred to Dr. Collins), sent him (Read), 20 or more letters. (Ex. 23.)

This is singular. Perhaps the reader can judge why they should send to Mr. Read when referred to Dr. Collins.

Mr. Read says the new piece of Mr. Ludlow's was the *best he ever saw*. (Ex. 24 and 26.)

This means, best for Mr. Read, and not, as might be supposed, the best for Dr. Collins.

Mr. Read says he thinks Dr. Collins will be pleased, when he sees Mr. Ludlow's article. (Ex. 26.)

Mr. Read was mistaken.

Mr. Read says he was requested by Mr. Ludlow to advise all Opium Eaters to take Dr Collins' Antidote. (Ex. 28.)

It is in proof that Mr. Read has advised the use of *other medicines* upon the face of Mr. Ludlow's article.

Mr. Read says he *does not know why Dr. Collins was not referred to in the Harper article.* (Ex. 29.)

If the reader can force himself to believe this he may

Mr. Read says that Dr. Collins *receives all the benefit* arising from Mr. Ludlow's article. (Ex. 30.)

Mr. Read is mistaken. It *is in proof* that Mr. Read *has charged Opium Eaters One Hundred Dollars* ($100.) *for medicine for which he has paid Dr. Collins Fifty Dollars* ($50.)

Fifty Dollars a piece for patients sent to Dr. Collins, might be called disinterested philanthropy —but it isn't very often.

———o———

The following from the facile pen of Mr. FITZ HUGH LUDLOW is taken from Harper's Easy Chair for August, 1870, and is the article to which reference has been made in the preceeding pages.

The reader will be loth to believe that Mr. Ludlow saw the false impressions which his article would create, and the long list of wrongs to which it would give rise. And surely no one can for a moment doubt that having seen the injustice which has been done, he will, to the best of his ability, see that honor is given to whom it is due, and justice done to all.

NEW YORK, June 15, 1870.

*Dear Easy Chair*:—To-day sailing for Europe, an invalid, with all the uncertainties of return which attend such a one, may I ask to say through you a word or two, in parting, to the class of our suffering fellow men and women for whom, as you know, I have spent a large part of my life—all that part, indeed, which is usually the leisure of a laborious profession?

In the book published two years since by the Messrs. Harper, under title of "The Opium Habit," whose earlier chapters were edited by, and the two closing ones original with me, I gave to the public as condensed a statement as my limits made imperative of the course of treatment which many years' medical and scientific study, together with an experience among Opium Eaters scarcely to be surpassed in extent, had taught me was the safest, quickest, least painful exit from a hell over whose interior penetralia at least Humanity had for years concurred to write, with a sigh, "Lasciate ogni speranza." There I showed the possibility of a release, and, so far as could be done in such broad touches, sketched the means. There I promised a salvation I had repeatedly seen effected, and accumulated all the incentives and encouragements to seek it which I knew; but with these I was obliged to preach a Spartan—say rather a Christian—courage such as few women and fewer men can summon to their aid in the protracted agonies of the contest by which the Opium Eater must win his freedom, even under the many palliating and relieving circumstances which I there revealed. I had not then found what I confess has been one of my life's ruling passions—a very *agony of seeking* to find—any means of bringing the habituated Opium Eater out of his horrible bondage, without, or comparatively without, pain. Thus far I had failed in my wrestling interrogations of Nature for the Antidote, the substitute, the agent, whatever it might be, by which Opium might be so gradually replaced and eradicated as to present the slave, some bright celestial morning, with his manumission, before he could feel the blows which struck the shackles from his feet.

I ask you, dear Easy Chair, to rejoice with me that, in all probability, that wonderful discovery has now been made; that henceforth the salvation of the Opium Eater, like that from any other chronic disease, may be accomplished in such a way that the cure brings not an increase but a relief of the original suffering; that the process of giving to him his new self may now be not a terrible volcanic throe that tears soul and body to pieces, but a gentle, painless change, like those milder forces of nature shown in the progress of the seasons, the unbinding of the frost, the return of the sun and gentle rains. A year ago I was almost in despair of such a blessing; but I must believe—must declare—what my eyes have looked upon.

I have had under my eyes a patient who had been an habitual user of opium for years—who daily rations of morphia had now reached the terrible amount of thirty grains, (a case quite astounding to minds not experienced among Opium Eaters, but having numerous parallels in my acquaintance)—who abandoned the drug at once in its every form, and never touched it again from that moment (four months ago) to the present time. I have seen him going on with his daily avocations, suffering no pain which required him to lie down for a single day, feeling no temptation to seek opiates, although he constantly carried about his old morphia powders on his person, and had made the un-Spartan resolve to resume his relief if the new experiment for a moment failed. He was expecting anguish all the time for his first month of trial; but it never came, has not come, and is most unlikely to come now that, after all these months his digestion has regained its vigor, his step its elasticity, his eyes and cheeks the freshness of health. Besides this case I have seen numerous others, when their various complications are considered, no less remarkable, and from many more have had letters, all joyfully unanimous in the testimony that their exit was painlessly accomplished, and that the opium-craving was not only appeased, but quite eradicated, by the process of cure. I have been compelled to confess that the life-long object of my search seemed most marvellously accomplished.

Were I staying in this country, instead of going abroad as my last chance for life and health, I would joyfully continue to answer the correspondence which floods me on this subject from all parts of the Union, and, at any expense to myself, make known this salvation to the most sorrowful sufferers of this world. Were this an article, instead of a communication receiving your hospitality, dear Easy Chair, and were *Harper's* a technical magazine, in which I could develop the process of substitution and elimination by which this marvellous blessing is accomplished, I would now speak more at length. It is now sufficient to say that the discovery is one which ranks in importance to human weal and woe with vaccination, chloroform, or any grandest achievement of beneficent science which marks an age. The many who can bear me witness how willingly I have responded to all inquiries for help to the Opium Eater, by visit or letter, will be glad to know that during my absence such inquirers may apply to my noble-hearted and philanthropic friend, Mr. Henry Read, of Lowell, Massachusetts, who possesses all my information on the subject, and has kindly consented to let me roll off upon his shoulders the loving but heavy burden of answering such questions as might, if I staid here, be addressed to me.

By lettting me say these parting words from your kindly elevation, my dear Easy Chair, you will bless thousands of sorrowful souls, and send one away to Europe far less sorrowful, because most hopeful, for them. Your friend,

FITZ HUGH LUDLOW.

#### OPIUM EATERS, ETC.

The following letter, bearing date San Francisco, Cal., Jan. 26, 1871, contains the personal experiences of a confirmed morphine eater, and exposes, in a clear and forcible manner, the determined effort of FITZ HUGH LUDLOW and HARPER'S MAGAZINE to wrest from Dr. Collins the honor and emoluments of his great discovery.

The Chicago "*Times*," in giving place to the article says :

"It exposes a very extraordinary attempt to defraud the discoverer of a wonderful remedy out of the just returns of his discovery, the parties to the transaction being a well-known literateur, who appears, according to the statements made, to have been abetted by the publishers of *Harper's Magazine*. The article will be perused with much interest."

The New Church "*Independent*," published at the home of Dr. Collins, in giving place to the article, says :

"We publish in this number of the *Independent* a letter, written by one of the patients of Dr. Collins, of this place, in reference to his Opium Antidote and the Doctor's treatment by the *Harper's*. We are assured that it is genuine and not a mere advertisement as some may suppose. In view of the *good* which we *know* has resulted from this treatment for the Opium Habit, we cheerfully make room for this letter. As the Doctor is an old citizen of our town and we have a personal acquaintance with him and two of the parties he has cured, we cheerfully recommend him to the slaves of Opium."

The New York *Independent* says:

"In more than four hundred cases the remedy of Dr. Collins has been thoroughly tested, *without a failure*, many of the cases treated having been in the last stages of the dreadful disease."

"The case of 'G. A. T.,' the history of which appeared in the Chicago *Times*, March 11th, is, without doubt, the most wonderful case upon record. *Sixty* grains of morphine was his daily portion; and yet at the first dose of the medicine all desire for the drug instantly ceased."

The *Argus*, published at La Porte, says:

"The article in the *Independent* will be read with interest, not only by those who are seeking relief from the slavery of Opium, but by all parties who feel that right should prevail and merit receive its just reward."

FITZ HUGH LUDLOW AND HARPER'S MAGAZINE.

Twenty-two years of age, with a constitution of iron, brave of heart and strong of limb, flushed with the brightest and highest of ambitions, and cheered on by the smiles and huzzas of the loyal people in the staid little town of

W——, I marched, in 1861, for the battle-fields of the South.

To be in the advance of our great army seemed ever to be my fortune, and until the fall of 1864 I had never left my command.

But worn out with the hardships at which, during the first two years of my service I had always laughed, I found myself, in September of 1864, *en route* for my home in Illinois.

But how was I changed! In the rude strength of youth, every inch of me a man, I had, scarcely three years before, left my home and my friends. I was returning to it and to them a mere wreck; an arm left upon the well-fought field of Shiloh; a bullet near my spine, the parting compliment of the day at Stone River; constitution broken, ambition gone, wasted to a shadow, and only sustained by the wonderful power of Opium.

Long weeks and longer months of suffering had so shattered my nervous system and reduced my strength, that as a *dernier resort* my physician had prescribed *Morphia*, and with the most flattering results. Soothed by the wonderful power of that most wonderful of narcotics, I forgot my pain, and if I did not really *enjoy* life, I *lived* and "blest the man that first invented Opium."

From June, 1864, until the winter of 1867, my pain had been soothed and my strength sustained by *Morphia*, the daily dose rapidly increasing from one grain to twenty-three grains.

Not sufficiently robust to endure the rigors of our northern climate, and having friends upon the Pacific coast, I moved in the autumn of '67 to the city of San Francisco, where I was first awakened from the deadly stupor in which I had so long lived. I had gained somewhat in weight and in strength, and the vigor and clearness of my mind had been unimpaired, and, little dreaming of the gulf that yawned before me, little dreaming of the shackles that bound me, for I had never moved to the full length of my chain,—I never hesitated when I put to my lips in the morning the drug that was to give me the strength for the day's labor. And why should I? For years I had leaned upon its power; for years it had soothed me when my body was racked with pain; it had been my *strength*, my *life*. Why should I fear that one day the most gentle of servants should become the most relentless of masters? No faithful friend warned me of the dangerous path I was treading. I was to learn the error of my way by the bitterest of all experiences.

The pursuit of my profession carried me to a small settlement in the interior of California, where, after a long ride of twelve hours, I found myself at a late hour one Saturday night.

Weary and cold I retired, only to be haunted by the most fearful of dreams, and to wake from them with a sense of utter exhaustion, and an uncontrollable desire for *some* thing. As hundreds of times before, I sought my *Morphia*, believing that in it I should find relief. My pockets were turned inside out, my valise ransacked for the precious drug, when, who shall describe my horror? it was out!

The late hour of the night, the insignificance of the settlement, not large enough, probably, to support a drug store, and the wildness of the storm and bad condition of the roads, shutting me out from the world, flashed upon my mind in an instant.

The house was aroused, and the country physician sent for in the hopes of finding that for which I was almost dying, but in vain.

The long day—the longest I had then known—was near its close; the messenger sent forty miles to procure *Morphia* had not returned, and with brain on fire I was raving like a mad man. The fearful sufferings of that day I shall not attempt to describe. There are those who have experienced such agony, whose pens are more ready than mine.

The *Morphia* came at last, and in the thirty grains which I so eagerly swallowed, I forgot the furnace through which I had passed.

This was my first awakening, and I was not slow to appreciate the depth of the gulf into which I had fallen; I was not slow to believe that I was the veriest of slaves, bound body and soul.

How my soul revolted at such bondage; how I struggled to free myself from my fetters; how I agonized—I pray God none may know.

Three different times I endeavored, unaided, to burst my bonds, but every time in vain, and after each trial I was compelled to increase my daily dose. Never relinquishing my desire to once more stand upon my feet a free man, I left no stone unturned to accomplish the end. Eminent physicians were consulted, and for different periods of time their advice followed; but the untold sufferings through which I was made to pass resulted only in the lessening of my strength and the chilling of my hopes.

An advertisement in a Memphis paper attracted my attention, and I applied to the advertiser, who claimed to have discovered a painless cure for the Opium Habit. His remedy was faithfully tried; I lived over again the terrible anguish which I can never forget, and seeing the great gate of doom closing upon me, the last flickering ray of hope expired, and taking *sixty* grains of *Morphia* per day, I gave myself over, body and soul, to that Tyrant as unrelenting as Death, and far less generous.

FITZ HUGH LUDLOW,
himself an Opium Eater, had turned his attention to the unhappy condition of the bondmen and bondwomen, and had published in *Harper's* his knowledge upon the subject, under the title of "What Shall They Do to be Saved?"

The article was in the usually brilliant style of that brilliant man, but my own experience had taught me the utter uselessness of his plan when applied to a case as desperate in all its phases as was my own.

I read a book, accredited, though erroneously, to him, entitled "The Opium Habit,"—but saw not one word calculated to arouse in my heart the shadow of a hope.

The months went on, and I was daily growing weaker under a punishment greater than I could bear, when the August number of *Harper's Magazine* was laid upon my table.

I took it up and mechanically glanced at its contents, as I lazily cut its pages. At last my eye fell upon an article which has probably been read by more Opium Eaters in this country than any other literary or scientific article ever written. I read and re-read, until the hope long dead underwent a gradual resurrection, until, as I laid down the book, its wings were wide spread.

Ludlow had really found what had been to him his "life's ruling passion;" he had unlocked the door that shut so many human beings out in the darkness of despair; he had made for himself a name second to that of no great benefactor of humanity—a name that our children's children should rise up and call blessed. I closed my eyes and, forgetting for a moment my misery, I fancied that I was free. I rose above the terrible slough of despond; I saw the shackles loosen and fall off, and, thanking God and Ludlow, I was happy.

But I could not always dream, and, waking once more to the dread realities with which I was surrounded, I resolved to lose no time in possessing myself of the wonderful Elixir of Life.

To the friend of Mr. Ludlow, Henry Read, of Lowell, Massachusetts, all anxious inquirers upon the subject were referred.

Mr. Reed was written to—my case minutely described, and any amount of money that might be demanded gladly tendered—not for a *cure*, that was *impossible*—but for even temporary relief from my anguish.

For days that lengthened into weeks, I impatiently awaited the mail that should bring me, perhaps, a word of encouragement—but it came not.

A telegraphic dispatch remaining unanswered added to the terrible suspense of my condition, and once more my hope was chilled.

Ludlow had sailed for Europe long before; a communication between his agent and myself could not be established—and what was I to do? But I could do anything but remain idle.

I had seen somewhere an article highly commendatory of the Antidote, but denying the truth of the statement that Ludlow was its discoverer.

Matters were becoming complicated, so I would write to the Easy Chair of *Harper's*—surely *it* knew all about it. I wrote, inclosing return postage, earnestly requesting that the name and residence of the discoverer be given me.

Weeks passed on, and, receiving no reply, and fearful that the letter had miscarried or been mislaid, I wrote another letter—a personal one—addressed to the Editor of the Easy Chair by name. The fate which had followed my other communications did not forget this one, and an answer was never received.

At about this time—November, 1870—there appeared in the Easy Chair an "Explanation," that explained nothing but served to complicate still more a complicated affair. It seemed to me that at least the name of the discoverer of the Remedy might have been mentioned, allowing Opium Eaters themselves to have determined regarding the "enormous prices" charged—a faculty which they possess in perhaps as high a degree as the occupant of the Easy Chair.

Painfully interested as I was, I could not fail to see that something was wrong—that somebody was endeavoring, from any motive save a good one, to withhold from Opium Eaters the name of their benefactor.

The conduct of *Harper's* plainly showed that Ludlow was not what he had claimed to be, and that the magazine was doing all in its power—not to rectify a glaring misrepresentation, but to clinch a falsehood and perpetuate a wrong.

Wrought up to a state of desperation which only a hopeless slave to Opium may know and feel, I once more wrote to the Easy Chair, entreating with all the eloquence and earnestness of misery that I might know to whom to apply for relief.

Fitz Hugh Ludlow was dead in Switzerland; Henry Read could not hear my cry; would the Easy Chair do this little act of kindness for humanity's sake? But the waste-basket of the Easy Chair was larger by half than its heart—and no reply was vouchsafed me.

The last week in November brought December *Harper*, and in the Easy Chair appeared an obituary upon Fitz Hugh Ludlow.

Here, at last, thought I, the mystery will be solved. If Ludlow be really the discoverer of this great cure, the fact cannot be omitted, and if he be not, how, in sketching his history, can his connection with the great remedy be passed by?

But the Easy Chair was careful to pass unnoticed a fact it long had hid, and the article to which thousands of Opium-Eaters, and scientific men everywhere, anxiously looked for a resolution of the problem amounted to—nothing.

Mr. Ludlow's article was not *frank,* said the Easy Chair, but it was not necessary to impute any ill-intent to the writer.

The real facts in the case, known as they must have been to the Easy Chair, were carefully withheld; the most important event in all the history of Ludlow's life was merely alluded to—and the mystery remained unsolved.

Surely, thought I, there is a part of the story yet untold; some motive very *deep*, if not very good, prompts the withholding of a single name, the divulging of which would bless thousands.

But the mystery was to be solved by and by —I was to be given to read the whole of the story, and to repeat it into listening and eager ears.

My condition at this time had become critical. Once more I had become but the shadow of a man—my brain and my body were racked by intensest pain—my days were full of agony and my nights of horror—and I had come to fear for the empire of my reason.

My physician and friends, one and all, had lost all hope, and were waiting for a summons they had long expected, and wondered at its long delay.

Sitting one day in the parlor of my home, for I had long ago given up my profession, my mail was brought in, and among it I found a little book sent to me by some sympathizing but unknown friend.

The title, "Theriaki and Their Last Dose," rather attracted my attention. Merely for the purpose of whiling away a half-hour, I commenced its perusal.

I soon became deeply interested, and read with increasing interest the letters of Fitz Hugh Ludlow, and the clear but astounding relation of the remarkable cures that had been performed.

Here then I had found what I had so long searched for—the name of the discoverer of the Antidote so carefully tested and strongly commended by Mr. Ludlow.

There remained in my mind no doubt as to whom the honor of the discovery belonged. This time Ludlow's letters were unequivocal, pointing directly to the man whose "thunder he had stolen"—with whose honor he had clothed himself. I read, and at once believed in the wonderful power of the Remedy, and believed that the man who could so vigorously conduct a warfare—surrounded as he was by difficulties almost insurmountable—to a successful termination, must surely have something for which to fight, could be anything but an impostor.

Ludlow, then, was not the discoverer of the Antidote, but, despite misrepresentations strengthened and aggravated by the conduct of the *Harper's*, the real discoverer had come to light in the person of Samuel B. Collins, of La Porte, Ind.

I exhibited the book to several of my most intimate friends, expressing my determination of sending at once for the medicine.

To this, however, my friends objected. I was so very low, they said, would it not be better to visit the Doctor in his own home? He would understand then, they argued, the desperate condition of my case.

Acting upon their earnest advice I prepared for what seemed to me a long, long journey, and one from which many of my friends never expected I would return alive. I reached Chicago, worn out by my trip, upon the 23d of December, 1870.

Needing rest, I concluded to remain one day in the city, and resolved, before I left, to call upon Mr. Chapman, whose name, as one of the cured Opium Eaters appears in "Theriaki."

I found Mr. Chapman an agreeable gentleman, and listened with intense interest to his relation of his sufferings and his cure; how for 14 years he had used 18 grains *Morphia* per day—and how he was completely and permanently cured. His assurance that in his opinion my cure was only a question of time, gave me greater confidence and stronger hope.

I reached La Porte Christmas eve, intending after a Sabbath day's rest to call upon the Doctor and lay my case before him.

A. P. Andrew, Jr., whose name also appears in "Theriaki," lived across the way from the hotel at which I was stopping, and upon him I called. He was the first person who ever took a dose of the Antidote, and was permanently cured in five months. Mr. Andrew corroborated the statements of Whitmore, Culver, and Darrow. Again

I was assured that my cure was not impossible, and, feeling sure that but a single night separated me from the mystery explained, I returned to the hotel.

The excitement which had thus far kept me up subsided now that I had reached the end of my journey, and I woke, upon the morning after Christmas, entirely exhausted.

Taking twenty-five grains of *Morphia* before I was able to leave my bed, I dressed, and wearily traversed the very short distance between the hotel and the residence of the Doctor.

I was ushered into a cozy little parlor, and in a moment the man in whose hands my destiny was held, appeared.

Picture to yourself a man, five feet ten inches in height, powerfully built,—long brown whiskers and mustache—light hair and complexion, and a light, piercing eye—a deliberate thinker and speaker—self-made and positive,—and you have the picture of the man who has solved the greatest of all medical problems—the discovery of a remedy which, in its power of benefiting humanity, is without a rival.

My case was quickly explained, and with bated breath I asked : " Can anything be done for me ?" The Doctor, in a tone of voice which plainly showed his wonderful confidence in the power of his remedy, slowly replied : " You have only to follow carefully all directions, and you can be cured painlessly—permanently." He paused a moment, as if for a reply, but I could say nothing.

"Your nerves, now shattered, will be strengthened," continued he, "the organs of your body resume their natural functions—and you will be a man again. It is only a question of time."

I was anxious to take the first dose of the medicine that promised to do so much for me, so I was requested to return to the office in the afternoon.

At just one o'clock, the time at which I usually took my dose of 15 grains, I returned to the office, and there took the first teaspoonful of the Antidote.

The effect was most wonderful; my nerves became instantly quiet—the temperature of my body regular and natural; in short, that single teaspoonful of medicine had completely taken the place of 15 grains of *Morphia*.

All that afternoon, like one in a dream, I wandered about—it surely could not be a reality—this freedom from pain! But two days passed and I had touched no *Morphia*, and felt better than I had felt for years.

Having nothing to call me home, I resolved to spend a week where I could be under the Doctor's own care, and during my visit to his home I related to him the many fruitless attempts I had made to discover his "habitation and his name," and how merely by accident I had finally made the discovery."

Evidently interested in the rehearsal of my trials, he gave me at length the facts of the case, placing in my hands copies of the documents necessary to substantiate the story.

That Opium Eaters may know the solution of a question which long has puzzled them, and in which they have a deep interest; that they may know the course pursued toward them by *Harper's Magazine*, and thus be able to distinguish their true friends, I shall briefly repeat the story:

The discovery of Dr. Collins was made in July, 1868, and upon the 18th day of the same month the first dose was taken by A. P. Andrew, Jr.

In the fall of the following year, though very little advertised, the fame of the remedy had traveled from mouth to mouth, until the Doctor had patients at many points distant from his home.

In October, 1869, a patient of the Doctor's residing in Missouri, sent to Fitz Hugh Ludlow a small phial of the Antidote, which he carefully tested. Mr. Ludlow then wrote to the doctor, Nov. 25, and a correspondence, interrupted only by Mr. Ludlow's departure for Europe, was the result. Mr. Ludlow desired to test the remedy, voluntarily promising, if the test was satisfactory, to write an article for both *Harper's Monthly* and *Weekly*, setting forth the facts in the case.

Dr. Collins furnished Mr. Ludlow with sixteen bottles of his medicine, free of charge; the test was carefully and successfully made, and Mr. Ludlow testified to *that* fact in his article published in August.

The article was written in June, and previous to its appearance a determined effort was made to form a copartnership between Ludlow, Reed, and the Doctor.

Negotiations of this nature being still pending, the long-looked-for article appeared, which rendered their favorable termination impossible, and betrayed the well-laid plan of defrauding the Doctor not only out of his hire, but out of the honor which was his due.

Believing, perhaps, in the probability of a partnership being formed, Ludlow had written the article in such a manner as to completely conceal the discoverer of the remedy, and place the honor upon himself.

So completely was Dr. Collins ignored, that his name was not mentioned, and Henry Read was named as the person to whom all inquirers should apply.

And to make room for this article, Mr. Ludlow withheld an advertisement designed for *Harper's*, and in which the name of Dr. Collins appeared.

But it is not necessary to impute any ill intent to the writer, says the Easy Chair—his " article was not as *frank* as it should have been "—but it was fully as frank as the Easy Chair's "Explanation" in November.

Then commenced the war with Mr Reed, who held, by the authority of Ludlow's article, the destinies of the discovery.

To correct the misrepresentations of Ludlow's article, and to wrest from Mr. Reed authority to which he was not entitled, "Theriaki" was published.

Mr. Reed, seeing to what his actions threatened to bring him, and tired perhaps, of the war, gracefully surrendered, and went at the work of righting the wrong. He used his influence with the Easy Chair to have the misrepresentation corrected, and the honor given to the real discoverer of the Remedy.

This the Easy Chair unconditionally promised to do, in the following letter, dated Sept. 5, 1870, and addressed to Henry Read:

"DEAR SIR: I have received both your last letters and have carefully considered what you say.

"It is too late to speak of the subject in the next number of the magazine, which is already in press; but in the following number I *shall state* upon your authority *that Mr. Collins* is the *inventor* and *proprietor;* that you and Mr. Ludlow testify to its efficacy; and that I, of course, cannot know whether you or he have any other than a philanthropic interest in it. That you have had such an interest hitherto, you say in your letters, although you also say it was for Ludlow's benefit. There is no harm in that, *but there is great harm in giving another impression, which Ludlow's letter certainly did.* Yours,

"(Signed),

"THE EASY CHAIR OF HARPER'S MAGAZINE."

There are two points in this letter worthy of mention: The direct promise to state that Dr. Collins was "the inventor and proprietor,"—and the honest indignation against the wrong impression conveyed by Ludlow's letter.

Mr. Read, having written Dr. Collins to the effect that the correction would be made, the doctor forwarded that portion of the letter to the "Easy Chair."

In the reply the Easy Chair forgets its unequivocal promise, but still expresses indignation at the deception:

"Sept. 27, '70.—The Easy Chair of *Harper's Magazine* has read Mr. Collins' note and inclosure.

"Long before, however, it had decided, upon further consideration, *not* to advertise Mr. Collins as the proprietor of the Antidote mentioned by Mr. Ludlow in an article which the Easy Chair would not have inserted had it been as fully informed upon the subject as it now is."

This much for the *promise* of the Easy Chair of *Harper's Magazine.*

Although perfectly aware of the deception that had been used,—by no means ignorant of the injury that had been done—and still crying out against it,—any just explanation of the matter was refused.

Well, the November number of *Harper* appeared and in it there was an "Explanation."

Again the name of Dr. Collins was omitted, though the Easy Chair knew the *facts*—and an attempt made to cast an air of suspicion around the whole matter—a statement being made in regard to the amount charged, which was in letter and in spirit a glaring falsehood. So much for the promise and "Explanation" of the Easy Chair. to right the wrong.

The importance of the matter, both to Dr. Collins and to Opium Eaters everywhere, demanded that at least one more attempt be made.

Moral suasion had entirely failed—no appeals from suffering humanity, no considerations of justice or of right, whatever, could move the Easy Chair—it now remained to try money.

Dr. Collins then wrote to the Easy Chair, inclosing fifty dollars,—briefly reviewing the facts *already known* to its occupant,—and concluding: "I have to request that you would, in your own way, and *no matter how briefly*, set this matter at rest, once and forever, by giving through the Easy Chair the credit of the discovery to whom it rightly belongs. This no less for the benefit of Opium Eaters than to further my own interests."

The result was the following letter, which plainly showed that not money even would incline the Easy Chair to do a simple act of justice:

NEW YORK, Oct. 24, 1870.—SIR: I have a note from you of the 17th inst., inclosing a money order for $50, and you request that certain things shall be stated in this department of the magazine.

"The late Mr. Ludlow wrote a note which was published in that department, alluding to an Opium Antidote, and mentioning Mr. Henry Read, of Lowell, as the person to be inquired of.

"What arrangements Mr. Ludlow and Mr. Read may have had, the Easy Chair does not know. *But no assertion whatever has been made in regard to you,* nor does the Easy Chair propose to make any—certainly not in consideration of money.

"Advertisements should be addressed to the publisher of the magazine.

"I inclose to you the money sent by you.

"Yours,

"(Signed)

"THE EASY CHAIR OF HARPER'S MAGAZINE."

Under date of September 5, the Easy Chair promised to state that Dr. Collins was the discoverer of the Antidote. Under date of October 24, no statement whatever had been made regarding him. If consistency be a jewel, the Easy Chair would make a good *setting.*

It became evident that the Easy Chair occupied a position entirely out of sight of the Scales of Justice, and the Doctor, as a last resort, forwarded to Harper & Bros., an advertisement, which, on account of its peculiarly objectionable "nature," I reproduce here:

"THE OPIUM HABIT.

"Fitz Hugh Ludlow's letters upon the subject of the Opium Habit, together with a full explanation of the discovery referred to by him in the August number of this magazine,—"Theriaki and their Last Dose,"—will be sent to any address free of charge.

"Address the discoverer of the Antidote,
"SAMUEL B. COLLINS, etc."

This advertisement was mailed upon the 1st of December. No acknowledgment of its receipt having been received, a letter of inquiry was mailed upon the 12th.

No notice having been taken of either letter, a telegram was sent upon the 19th, which elicited the following, to which the attention of Opium Eaters is called:

"NEW YORK, Dec. 20.—S. B. COLLINS: Advertisements of *such a nature*, don't wish to insert. (Signed) HARPER & BROS.

This, then, was the end of the whole matter. A gross misrepresentation had been made in the columns of the Easy Chair—that department of the magazine, though entirely cognizant of the fact, refused to make the correction,—forcing another misrepresenation upon the heels of a promise to rectify—and finally declining to insert for money an advertisement on " account of its nature,"—fully as unexceptionable as any that has ever appeared in the columns of that very select magazine.

And thus ends the story, interesting inasmuch as it proves the disinterested humanity of the Easy Chair, and its unfaltering devotion to what it believes to be right.

Poorly told as it has necessarily been, it may furnish food for reflection for those poor souls who have been misled as I was misled, and caused to suffer as I suffered, by an act of injustice, which a single word could have made right.

As for me, the Easy Chair, in giving place to Ludlow's article, had brightened my hope and lightened my heart, but it cruelly dashed my hopes, and I turned from it with a heavier feeling at my heart than I had ever known before.

For the harbor which I finally reached, for the smiling sky and quiet sea above and around me, I cannot thank *Harper*—for I reached that harbor despite the false lights that were ranged along the shore.

I remained in La Porte one week, and, taking a supply of medicine sufficient to effect a cure, I started for my home anything but the hollow-hearted ghost that the quiet Hoosiers stared at with mouths wide open.

It has now been thirty days since I touched a grain of *Morphia*, and I have gained so wonderfully in weight, in strength, and in looks that my friends are wont to pass me by unrecognized.

Because of the fulness of my heart, and that other poor souls may know and feel my happiness, this letter is written—and that said, my whole interest in the matter is told.

G. A. T.

Since the issuance of the first edition of "Theriaki," the number of patients has steadily increased, until there now stand upon the books nearly six hundred names.

Persons of all ages and conditions of life— strong men and weak women—persons afflicted with almost every ill to which flesh is heir, have been treated and cured, and so very many of the questions which patients would be led to ask may be anticipated in these pages.

There are some who, when they find that from the first dose of the Antidote all desire and necessity for Opium in any form disappear, become fearful that they are still using in some form or other, the drug from whose baneful influence they would escape.

If the fact that Opium does not antidote itself be borne in mind, and the patient remembers that no painless process of gradual diminution has ever been discovered, the idea will be at once dismissed.

To bring the patient from under the power of Opium *without pain*, requires that the undue tension of the nervous system be not too suddenly lessened, and so, as the drug is suddenly withdrawn, the Antidote supplies for the time being, its place, at the same time expelling the poison from the system, and restoring its nervous energies.

The Antidote holds the nervous system in the same condition of rest or unrest in which it finds it—lessening its tension so gradually as to be imperceptible to the patient.

Local and transient causes have their effects upon the strongest—there are times when we all feel languid and despondent—and to no person do these uncomfortable feelings come oftener than to the confirmed Opium Eater.

A patient while undergoing treatment most generally watches with the greatest anxiety the progress of the cure—is particularly sensitive to every change of feeling—and so is very apt to give great prominence to a symptom which at other times would pass unnoticed.

It is not strange that in the great process of elimination, and before the organs of the body have resumed their functions, the patient should feel at times a sensation of weariness—a lack of ambition.

But as no actual pain is felt, and as such symptoms are always transient, the patient should by no means lose courage in the efficacy of the Antidote.

There have been two instances where an oversensitive patient, experiencing this feeling of lassitude, has laid aside the Antidote and again resorted to Opium. A most unfortunate combination of circumstances has at once appeared—for while the Antidote is a perfect substitute for Opium, Opium is *not* a perfect substitute for the Antidote.

It sometimes happens that patients, feeling under the invigorating influence of the Antidote an increase of nervous power to which they have long been strangers, labor or exercise beyond their strength, thus bringing on a relaxed condition of the nervous system. At such times they occasionally complain that the Antidote has not sufficient *sustaining power*.

Dr. Collins wishes it understood that while the ordinary affairs of every-day life need not be interrupted during treatment, the medicine is not designed to furnish strength for unusual labor.

While Dr. Collins guarantees a cure in every case in which all directions are scrupulously followed, he wishes it distinctly understood that he neither guarantees a cure, or holds himself *in any way* responsible for any evil effects which might result from a violation of his explicit directions. Dr. Collins wishes here to warn patients from allowing any parties, whether Opium Eaters or not, to take, or even taste, the medicine prepared for another.

To save a multiplicity of questions, and that patients may never be at a loss to know what is expected of them, it is thought best to give the following

### DIRECTIONS.

Opium in every form must be entirely discontinued from the first dose of the Antidote, and never, under any circumstances whatever, be resorted to again.

All acids—including, of course, fruits that are sour, and all spirituous or malt liquors, must be entirely avoided.

The use in any form whatever of Mercury, Strychnia, Arsenic and Belladonna, is strictly forbidden

Mineral Waters, Sedlitz Powders, Hydrate Chloral and preparations of Indian Hemp, are also forbidden.

Should it any time become necessary to employ the services of a physician, the patient should particularly warn him against the use of any article above mentioned.

The doses are to be taken with regularity, and exactly as directed upon each label—and should never be increased or diminished except by direction of Dr. Collins.

Should the patient be troubled with constipation, the action of the bowels may be regulated by the use of from one to three of Tilden's Improved Cathartic Pills. Where the Pills cannot be obtained, the patient may use any mild cathartic which does not contain Calomel.

Diarrhea, which seldom occurs during treatment, may be checked with the following prescription:

Tinct. Capsicum ................................ 1 ounce.
Tinct. Myrrh .................................... 1 drachm.
Tannic Acid .................................... 10 grains.
Simple Syrup ................................... 3 ounces.

Mix. Dose: Twenty drops to a Teaspoonful every three hours.

Never doubting in the ultimate result of the treatment, let the patient be hopeful—following, with the utmost care, the directions given.

## TO PERSONS ORDERING MEDICINE.

It is not strange that there are many counterfeits before the public—medicines which, in *color* and *taste* resemble very closely the medicine compounded by Dr. Collins.

Such a medicine, but devoid, of course, of the wonderful powers of the genuine Antidote, is compounded in the city of La Porte.

That patients may not be imposed upon, the Doctor has taken precaution to have his name blown in the glass of each bottle, and to enclose in each box containing the *first* supply of medicine to each patient, a copy of Theriaki.

The patient, by remembering this, may avoid imposition: None genuine unless the words, "Opium Habit Cured by Dr. S. B. Collins, La Porte, Inda.," appear blown in the glass of each bottle—and a copy of Thériaki accompanies each first shipment.

From the price list given in these pages, there will be no deviation, it having been found necessary to work closely to an established rule.

In cases of absolute poverty, the person should obtain from near neighbors a sworn certificate of his or her circumstances, without which, no appeal for a reduction of price will be considered.

It should be remembered that the person should state the *full* amount of the drug necessary to keep the nerves in a perfectly quiet state, for when a *less* amount is given, the medicine fails to have any beneficial effect.

A blank containing questions to be answered is sent to each patient, with the request that it be filled out and returned.

Five dollars per bottle should accompany each order when medicine is to be sent, C. O. D.

Money sent by Post Office Order is always safe. When that cannot be done the letter should be registered.

All bills are payable monthly in advance.

Patients should always give County and State plainly.

Address

Dr. Samuel B. Collins,
La Porte, Ind.

If individual success only awakened honest emulation and quickened to honorable rivalry, this would be a very pleasant world. But envy, detraction and double dealing are called into life by that same success, just as the sun that ripens the corn gives rank luxuriance to the weeds between. Now Dr. Collins is the pioneer in the cure of the Opium Habit, his merits are recognized and rewarded, and it is wonderful to see how the little city of La Porte is astir with philanthropists who have given years, if not whole ages, to the discovery of an antidote for the great enslaver of the human race, to-wit, Opium, and have succeeded. Pamphlets with as many pages as there are days in a fortnight, come out like leaves in spring, proclaiming a year of jubilee to the hopeless victims abroad, forgetting all the while that "charity begins at home;" forgetting, if not the injunction "physician, heal thyself," at least the homely counsel, "physician, heal THINE OWN!" One comes reluctantly (!) before the public, clothed with modesty as with a garment, at the earnest solicitation of friends who have importuned and worried him outright into rescuing poppy-eating mankind. Antique professors come to resurrection and declare the new salvation. You can hardly turn over a mossy stone without finding a philanthropist under it.

## THE CRITERION OF MERIT.

They all bleed for suffering humanity, and shall not suffering humanity bleed a little in return? They extend bottles of blessing to the human race with one hand, but they throw boulders at Dr. Collins with the other. One name with a title at both ends, like an elephant, asserts that Dr. Collins is "not reliable," to which Dr. C. replies that the name aforesaid cannot be surpassed for *relie*-ability. All persons are not alike gifted, but Dr. C. is content. He is glad the old fashion of sacrificing a cock to Aesculapius is obsolete, else the philanthropists of La Porte, each claiming a bird for his especial offering, would be fatal to the poultry of La Porte.

But Dr. Collins has work much too serious and important to trifle by the way with philanthropists who have nothing to do but save mankind, while Dr. Collins has not only to cure the Opium Habit, but also to make money. He only wonders how whole life times of profound research for the discovery of an Opium cure should have ripened simultaneously, and only after Dr. Collins' success was fully assured. But there being no pecuniary advantage in the solution of this mystery, Dr. C. leaves it altogether to the philanthropists themselves.

Dr. Collins takes this method of announcing that he has made arrangements to erect at once a first class, three story marble front building, containing a laboratory and spacious offices and consultation rooms on EAST MAIN Street, POST OFFICE BLOCK in the city of LA PORTE. The vast increase of his professional business has compelled him to devise greater facilities for preparing the medicine and meeting the wants of his patients. When the new headquarters for the cure of the Opium Habit are completed, DR. COLLINS will be glad to welcome his friends, and if he can render the philanthropists any service, they need only drop the boulders outside the door while they extend to him the empty and friendly hand, and he will do any neighborly thing for them except disclosing the composition of the ONLY painless and certain remedy ever discovered —DR. COLLINS' OPIUM CURE.

## WHAT PATIENTS SAY.

The following from A. P. Andrew, Jr., who is one of the oldest, as he is one of the most respected citizens of La Porte, speaks for itself:

"LA PORTE, April 20, 1871.

" Dr. S. B. COLLINS :

Many persons have written to me wishing to know if the *cure* performed by the Compound prepared by you for the Opium Habit *sticks*, or in other words, stands the *test of time*.

It is now nearly two and a half years since I was *cured*, during which time I have not used Opium in any of its preparations, nor any substitute therefor—and have no inclination to do so. My health is good for one of my age—(seventy years). You can make such use of this as you please. Respectfully, etc.,

A. P. ANDREW, JR."

" HASTINGS, Mich., March 5, 1871.

" Dr. S. B. COLLINS—*Dear Sir :*

I am most happy to inform you that through the agency of your medicine I am at last cured of the Opium Habit. I do not feel the least desire for or need of Opium in any form ; and it is now nearly three weeks since I left off taking the substitute. I have about a bottle and a quarter left from the last three you sent me. I weigh thirty pounds more than I did a year ago, and am still gaining. My wife thinks I had better consult you about a substitute for ham and eggs; she says I keep her busy cooking. I hardly know how to express myself, I feel so different and so much more like my old self; and, above all, I feel myself no longer a *slave*.

But no one could appreciate how I feel, if I could tell it ever so well, except those who have been in a similar situation, and suddenly found themselves restored to life, health, and manhood again; and that, too, without any pain or inconvenience. Very truly yours,

J. C. KETCHUM."

I hereby certify that the following are true excerpta from original and genuine letters, now on file in my office, from patients whom I have treated, or am now treating for the Opium Habit.

SAMUEL B. COLLINS.

Sworn and subscribed to before me, the undersigned Justice of the Peace, the 24th day of April, 1871. J. FRADENBURG, J. P.

A lady patient in Connecticut writes:

"My head has not been so clear for years. I rest better nights and have a better appetite. I am entirely weaned from *Morphia*, and don't think I could be tempted to ever taste it again. You may well say that your medicine is the most wonderful discovery of the age—for it is indeed. There can't be praise enough for it."

A lady patient residing in Illinois writes:

"Your remedy is more than in my wildest dreams I had ever promised myself. I find it every thing, and if possible more, than you claim for it. I am doing very nicely, and shall ever hear your name with a throb of gratitude in my heart. I feel a deep interest in this matter—a strong desire that the unfortunate class of beings to whom I so lately belonged may be led to a knowledge of the aid you can give them."

A gentleman from Tennessee writes:

"I must confess my astonishment at the perfect results of the Antidote. From the first day to the present I can see an improvement in health and also in mind. That lost and anxious look has disappeared, and I am again cheerful and happy."

A gentleman residing in Michigan, after twenty-five years' habitual use of Opium, writes:

"I am a week old to-day, and behold, all things are new! Oh, marvellous discovery! You have that in your keeping more precious than the 'golden fleece' or the philosopher's stone, which were sought for so long and sought in vain! The good hand of our God has put in your hand a very Elixir of Life. I was never so happy—never so well in my life.

"To no man living have I so grateful a sense of debt as to you, for you cannot weigh out the price thereof in gold; it is not a debt of dollars."

A gentleman residing in New York, after taking one bottle of the Antidote, writes:

"Your Opium Antidote is the wonder of the age. I left off taking *Morphia* and began taking the Antidote, experiencing no bad feelings. I slept well each night, and had a good appetite all the time. The half has never been told of the wonderful properties of the medicine. I had tried different times to break myself of the habit, but failed each time, and suffered more than a person with the *delirium tremens*. But I am fully cured, and feel an hundred per cent. better than when taking *Morphia*."

A physician of eminence in Virginia writes:

"Your compound seems to contain everything requisite for the broken down, sensitive system of the Opium Eater. It works like magic in its sustaining, invigorating, and tranquilizing effects upon a worn out system, all of which properties are essential in such a curative, and are most harmoniously blended.

"I regard it as a substitute, antidote, and the finest stimulant I have ever known. It satisfies and gratifies the cravings for stimulants without producing the usual disagreeable after consequences."

A distinguished lawyer of Rhode Island, writes:

"I have never suffered for a single moment, and the only difficulty I find is to *think* of it and take the medicine regularly. I feel perfectly satisfied, and perfectly well. The past winter has been one of unusual trial to me. I have been in Court almost every day without exception, since I commenced taking the medicine. I feel perfectly clear, and can bear *any amount* of fatigue and hard brain work.

"Say to the world that it is the *greatest*, most wonderful and most priceless boon and discovery ever offered to suffering humanity in this or any other age."

From Indiana a patient writes:

"Thanks be to God, dear Sir, for your wonderful and painless cure—for it *is* painless in the strictest sense, I having felt better *every* way, from the first dose—*much* better than when in regular use of the wily drug. My skin cleared up—my eyes brightened, and what was still better my original *elasticity* and *clearness* of intellect returned to me. My sleep became natural and refreshing—no more twitching of my nerves, and starting up in my sleep—my appetite constantly improving, sensibility of my bowels returning— all my secretions resuming a normal character. In a word, I feel like a new man—am made over—becoming *young again*."

## WHAT THE PRESS SAYS.

The remedy of Dr. Collins has been tested in hundreds of cases without a single failure, and Fitz Hugh Ludlow, after thoroughly testing it, declared it to be the most wonderful discovery of the nineteenth century.—*Buffalo Courier.*

Dr. Collins, as the discoverer of a painless cure for the Opium habit, has conferred as great a blessing upon humanity as did Jenner in his discovery of vaccination, or Guthrie in his discovery of chloroform.—*Chicago Journal.*

It is known that the greatest efforts have been put forth to find some remedy or help by which the terrible victims of the Opium habit might be enabled to get rid of their chains. The result had been, till lately, like the search for the *elixir of life*—all in vain. Fitz Hugh Ludlow—himself a victim—says, "it had been his life's ruling passion, a very agony of seeking to find some antidote for the evil." In vain DeQuincy, another illustrious victim, wailed out, "the chain must be loosed and unwound, link by link, from the end back to the beginning; and not one in ten thousand is able to endure the prolonged anguish. Nature has yielded her secret. Help has come,—perfect, complete, painless.— *Herald, Leslie, Mich.*

OPIUM.—The honor of the discovery of Chloroform— assuredly one of the most beneficent discoveries ever made in medicine—must be shared between Guthrie, Soubeiran and Leibig, each having discovered it at about the same time, in the year 1831.

But in 1868 a discovery was made which in its power of benefiting humanity is not second to Chloroform, and which for years has defied the unwearied search of some of the most eminent of medical men.

We refer to the discovery of Dr. SAMUEL B. COLLINS, of La Porte, Ind., a *painless cure* for the Opium Habit.—*N. Y. Independent.*

## WHAT THE PRESS SAYS.

In the April number of the New Church *Independent* is published a letter from California, detailing a history of the trials of one of our townsmen, in his efforts to prevent Fitz Hugh Ludlow—a writer for Harper's Magazine—from swindling him out of the benefits arising from the discovery of a very important medicine, for the cure of the Opium Habit. The fact of the discovery is well known to nearly all of our local readers, but the course pursued by Eastern sharpers to swindle Dr. Collins is known to but few, and the article in the *Independent* will be read with interest, not only by those who are seeking relief from the slavery of Opium, but by all parties who feel that right should prevail and merit receive its just reward. Dr. C. made this discovery in the summer of 1868, but his circumstances were not such as to enable him to bring it immediately before the public. By some *hocus pocus* the great Fitz Hugh Ludlow, who was himself an Opium Eater, learned the efficacy of the medicine, and deliberately planned to cheat Dr. Collins out of the honors and emoluments justly his due. But we are happy to chronicle the fact that he met with signal failure. His schemes were completely thwarted, and the Doctor remains in undisturbed enjoyment of the fruits of his great discovery. His business is rapidly increasing and he has the perfect confidence of an immense number of patients and correspondents. His success is a feather in the cap of La Porte, and his course will teach Eastern sharpers to seek victims elsewhere than in our little Forrest city.—*La Porte Argus.*

enclosing a small pamphlet prepared by somebody in La Porte, who is ambitious to be a boon to his fellow-beings.

Of the pamphlet and the pamphleteer, Dr. COLLINS has only to say that the pamphleteer in question might, perhaps, find fit subjects for his wonderful skill within his own immediate family.

But the *Doctor* deems it an act of justice to his patients to assure them that however names have been obtained by the person in question, it has certainly been after the packages bearing those names have left the Doctor's office and passed into the custody of the Express Company; and to state further that he has taken such measures as will effectually prevent any tampering with his private correspondence in the future.

www.ingramcontent.com/pod-product-compliance
Lightning Source LLC
Chambersburg PA
CBHW030407170426
43202CB00010B/1522